W9-BMV-376

Share Your Master's Happiness

Share Your Master's Happiness

Dr. Glenn Parkinson

iUniverse, Inc.
New York Lincoln Shanghai

Share Your Master's Happiness

Copyright © 2005 by Glenn R. Parkinson

All rights reserved. No part of this book may be used or reproduced by any means, graphic, electronic, or mechanical, including photocopying, recording, taping or by any information storage retrieval system without the written permission of the publisher except in the case of brief quotations embodied in critical articles and reviews.

iUniverse books may be ordered through booksellers or by contacting:

iUniverse
2021 Pine Lake Road, Suite 100
Lincoln, NE 68512
www.iuniverse.com
1-800-Authors (1-800-288-4677)

Scripture taken from the HOLY BIBLE, NEW INTERNATIONAL VERSION®. NIV®. Copyright©1973, 1978, 1984 by International Bible Society. Used by permission of Zondervan.

ISBN-13: 978-0-595-35492-4 (pbk)
ISBN-13: 978-0-595-79983-1 (ebk)
ISBN-10: 0-595-35492-0 (pbk)
ISBN-10: 0-595-79983-3 (ebk)

Printed in the United States of America

to a congregation I love,
Severna Park Evangelical Presbyterian (PCA)

Contents

Acknowledgments

Preaching is a great joy. Getting into print some series that are special to me is an extra blessing. This could never have happened without a lot of help. My wife, Micki, not only edits my written work, but she was a tremendous partner in developing the original messages. She also designed the cover. Her creativity and wisdom are amazing. Flo Wolfe once again gave her critical and very helpful expertise to the project. Many thanks to Ana Bangs for initially getting my notes into useable form, and to Susan Whaley for the photograph on the back cover. Of course, I am again grateful to God for my friends, brothers and sisters, Session and pastoral associates at SPEP. They make pastoring a joy.

Good and Faithful Servant

o o o o o o o o o o o o o o o o o o o o o o o o o o o o o o o o o

"Again, it will be like a man going on a journey, who called his servants and entrusted his property to them. To one he gave five talents of money, to another two talents, and to another one talent, each according to his ability. Then he went on his journey. The man who had received the five talents went at once and put his money to work and gained five more. So also, the one with the two talents gained two more. But the man who had received the one talent went off, dug a hole in the ground and hid his master's money.

"After a long time the master of those servants returned and settled accounts with them. The man who had received the five talents brought the other five. 'Master,' he said, 'you entrusted me with five talents. See, I have gained five more.' "His master replied, 'Well done, good and faithful servant! You have been faithful with a few things; I will put you in charge of many things. Come and share your master's happiness!' "The man with the two talents also came. 'Master,' he said, 'you entrusted me with two talents; see, I have gained two more.' "His master replied, 'Well done, good and faithful servant! You have been faithful with a few things; I will put you in charge of many things. Come and share your master's happiness!' "Then the man who had received the one talent came. 'Master,' he said, 'I knew that you are a hard man, harvesting where you have not sown and gathering where you have not scattered seed. So I was afraid and went out and hid your talent in the ground. See, here is what belongs to you.' "His master replied, 'You wicked, lazy servant! So you knew that I harvest where I have not sown and gather where I have not scattered seed? Well then, you should have put my money on deposit with the bankers, so that when I returned I would have received it back with interest. "'Take the talent from him and give it to the one who has the ten talents. For everyone who has will be given more, and he will have an abundance. Whoever does not have, even what he has will be taken from him. And throw that worthless servant outside, into the darkness, where there will be weeping and gnashing of teeth.'"

—Matthew 25:14-30

Stewardship is a biblical image taken from life to illustrate spiritual principles and responsibilities. A steward was a kind of household servant, the servant who was in charge, with the responsibility and authority to represent the homeowner. Most businesses operated out of the home or estate, so stewards also functioned as business managers. In the Old Testament, Jacob and Joseph both functioned as stewards at different times. We see stewards in charge of funds, property, and children. Abraham's steward was even responsible for finding a wife for Isaac.

By the time of Christ, every household of distinction had a steward. Some were slaves, some were free. Stewards supervised the family business, paid workers, looked after other servants, and sometimes saw to the education of the children. They were treated more as partners, carefully chosen for positions of great trust. Think of how carefully we choose a babysitter, a school, a lawyer or a CPA. A steward could be all these things, and more, rolled into one.

Many of Jesus' parables involved servants who functioned as stewards. Jesus would refer to God or to Himself as a master, and then talk to His disciples about how they were to view their lives as His stewards managing the work—or the people—He was entrusting to them. To keep things simple, He sometimes used money as a convenient symbol for the full range of a steward's responsibilities.

We begin our study with Matthew 25 because this parable not only uses ideas from stewardship to make a point; it virtually defines what stewardship is all about. That's our goal in this chapter: to come up with a definition of stewardship that we can use throughout this study.

On Assignment

The parables of Matthew 25 follow Jesus' teaching about His future return from heaven. These stories about "the kingdom of heaven" teach Christ's disciples how we should prepare for His return. Our text begins, "it will be like a man going on a journey…" Jesus was, indeed, approaching the final journey that had prompted His incarnation and birth. At the Passover just a few days away, Jesus will tell them, "I came from the Father and entered the world; now I am leaving the world and going back to the Father." (John 16:28). After the cross and resurrection, He will ascend to heaven and be gone from them. When Jesus states in our parable, "After a long time the master of those servants returned," He is referring to His second coming at the end of history.

In this story, Jesus compares Himself to a wealthy man who goes on an extended journey and gives eight talents of his wealth to three servants to manage in his absence. We know that Jesus wants us to think of this man as wealthy because we are told he has several servants, and he distributes a great sum of money. A *talent* was a measure of currency. One talent would have taken an average laborer 20 years to earn. With so much money involved, the master takes each servant's abilities into account. He gives five talents to one, two to another, and one to the third. Clearly, he has different expectations concerning what each one can produce. But just as clearly, he expects each one to do his best, and he plans to reward them accordingly.

"After a long time the master of those servants returned and settled accounts with them." Remember, it is the master's money we're talking about, not the servants'. The master wants his capital back, of course. And he is very interested to see what the servants have accomplished with the money he invested in them. Two servants approach the master with obvious delight. The original Greek text sounds like, "Master, five talents you gave me—here's five more!" Or "Two talents you gave me—here's two more!" There's obvious excitement as the servants cry out, "See!", "Look!" You can see them smiling as they lay down the fruit of their labor. The first two servants are obviously happy to see their master, and delighted to give him back more than he left with them. In response, the master is also delighted. But notice, he doesn't focus on the money. He doesn't say, "Wow, I'm richer!" He says, "Well done, good and faithful servant! You have been faithful." Then he allocates a very generous reward.

The situation is quite different, of course, with the third servant. The third servant has buried the master's money for safekeeping, and simply returns it to him. Even though the amount of money is much less than that handled by the other two, the master's reaction is nonetheless quite severe, as if it wasn't the money per se that he is concerned about. The third servant gives a little speech, explaining that he knew the master would just take away any profit he earned. So, since the servant wouldn't benefit from his labor, he just wanted to make sure the master got all his money back in one piece. The master is clearly disappointed. The way this is written, it seems as if he is hurt or offended by the way the third servant speaks about him, as "a hard man who profits off the labor of others." The master calls this servant wicked because of the way he talks about him. Lazy as well, for his unwillingness to work for the master's profit. He no longer wishes to employ this man; the third servant is fired.

At this point, we are reminded again that this parable is really about when Christ returns and settles accounts with everyone in final judgment. The language used for firing this guy is the language of Hell. "Throw that worthless servant outside, into the darkness, where there will be weeping and gnashing of teeth." Contrast this with the joy offered the other two servants (in a spirit that reminds us of the wedding feast mentioned in the parable just before this one), and we understand that the third servant represents those cast into the outer darkness of Hell, while the first two represent those invited to the blessed feast of paradise.

What is this parable teaching? Surely, we are accountable to use what God has given us until Christ returns. We'll be rewarded if we do, and punished if we don't. That is all true, of course. Yet, it is a truth that still misses the heart and soul of the text.

What God is Looking for

When you consider the parable as a whole, it becomes clear that the master is not focused on the money. The return he gets on his investment is important, but it's important because of *what it reveals about the servants*. We've already noted that the master does not say anything about the money, per se. "Wow, now I have twice the money I started with." "Wow, now I can get that new chariot I've been thinking about!" You can almost see his gaze looking up from the bags of money deposited on his table, to the *man* standing before him. "Well done, good and faithful servant!" The master had three servants; which of them, if any, could he *really* count on? Which of them could he trust to be the kind of person he wanted as a principal business partner, someone he could work with on a permanent basis on really important matters?

To speak of "really important matters" may seem strange when these men were given a fortune to manage. But Jesus makes it very clear that this large sum they managed for limited time is *nothing* compared to the master's complete holdings. "Well done, good and faithful servant! You have been faithful with a *few* things; I will put you in charge of *many* things." In a similar parable, recorded in Luke 19, Jesus has the master say, "Well done, my good servant!…Because you have been trustworthy in a very small matter, take charge of ten *cities*.'"

Fortunes are relative. We have today in America what seems like a fortune at our disposal: nice homes, children we love, fine electronics, savings and investments for retirement. Compared to most other people around the world and throughout history, we certainly are well off. But the things we manage in this life, even though they may seem like a fortune to us now, are small, almost insignificant, when compared to what trusted servants *will* manage when Christ returns to manage the rebuilding of the entire earth.

The Apostle Paul speaks of an eternal glory that far outweighs anything in this life. In the last chapter of this study, we will look again at the world, or age, that is coming. But even here at the beginning, we can immediately appreciate the sense of proportion Jesus describes. Eight talents given to invest, 48,000 denars, 160 years of annual wages. But for this master, even this large sum is *small potatoes*; he called it managing a "few things." What he was really interested in—and friends, this is what you have to see to understand this parable—what the master was really interested in was finding people he could ultimately trust to manage "many things." Or as he put it elsewhere, "many cities." The opportunities we have in this lifetime to accomplish God's will on earth as in heaven are crucially important, to be sure. But in terms of size, magnitude and glory, they are peanuts compared to what God and His people can build together in glory! This parable is not about producing a little extra income for the Lord. It's about God looking for servants today who can become faithful stewards tomorrow, people He wishes to entrust with His large family and great enterprise, His dreams and aspirations for mankind.

God's dreams and aspirations for mankind—we're talking about eternity here! Eternal life is not a stagnant thing, as if playing harps on clouds were meant to literally describe what we will do with our time. Imagine instead an eternity of building, growing, discovering, creating—an everlasting age in which sinless freedom is the *norm*, and the resources we have to build with are immense. In this parable, the master was not looking for a few extra bucks, a little more loose change. Rather, he designed an exercise to find men and women he could trust. Men and women with whom he wanted to build the most magnificent estate ever conceived! The kind of people you could trust to make entire cities great.

Make no mistake: our limited stewardship in this life is a test for much greater stewardship in the future. Salvation is a gift, but stewardship is a test. When Christ returns, every one of His people will stand before Him saved by grace, but each will also give an account of his/her stewardship. We will account for every single thing entrusted to us here: every person, every thing, every opportunity, every dollar, every day, every ability. Christ will examine how we have used what we were given to accomplish His will—like the master counting the bags of wealth laid on the table in front of Him.

But just like the master of the parable, He will really be looking at *us*. He doesn't expect us all to accomplish the same amount. He knows our abilities, and they differ. Frankly, He really isn't too excited about what we have accomplished, in and of itself, as if our small achievements would add all that much to what He already has. What He will be looking for is good and faithful servants.

Notice that He does not plan to reward them with some of the "gold," or some glory of their own. In the parable, the servants don't get to keep anything they earned; it all goes to the master. No, His reward is to hire them for positions of service in the *great* project, the one that towers over this world's greatest joys, the project that will just be getting warmed up 10 million years from now, the project that will never be finished, because it will continually top itself: the eternal kingdom of God. Good and faithful servants will be rewarded with an assignment of stewardship involving God's eternal glory. The bags of gold are important because they represent months and years of hard work. But they get put aside in the petty cash fund. The wealth which the master truly prizes on that day—what lights up his heart—is finding servants who will be good and faithful *stewards*.

The Heart of the Matter

There is one other important point in this parable, and it deals with what makes a good steward. At first glance, you might think it's simply the one who makes money for the master, the one who is effective in using what he has. He doesn't have to be as effective as someone else who has more God-given talent, but he has to be as fruitful as he possibly can. That is correct, of course, but it still misses the whole point Jesus is trying to make.

Think about the problem with the third servant. Why didn't he work hard with the money? Why didn't he at least give the money to bankers who would manage it for him and earn a little interest? The reason was that the third servant had no love for his master. "The man who had received the one talent came. 'Master,' he said, 'I knew that you are a hard man...'" A hard man? Cold? Unfeeling? Cruel? Unfair? Yes, that's it: unfair! "I knew that you are a hard man, harvesting where you have not sown and gathering where you have not scattered seed." To paraphrase: "Master, you like to profit from the work of others. We do all the work, and you get all the profit. We put in the labor, and you get all the glory. You act as if this business is all about you. Well, here is what you gave me, that's all I owe you. Now we're even."

To paraphrase the master's response: "Wait a minute! You think I am a hard boss because I think the business belongs to me? Listen, pal, this business *does* belong to me. You think I am cruel and unfair? I've given you millions of dollars to manage, from which you could take expenses. I've given you a salary on top of that. I have given you a nice home—my home—to live in, with my family. I have a feast ready to celebrate our joint venture. I'm prepared to offer partnerships to people who serve me well. You resent that the purpose of your work is to bring my glorious plans to life? Then, we're through. I don't want you working for me anymore. Give me your keys, clear out your desk and get out! I never want to see your face again."

Jesus describes the third servant as wicked and lazy. The man harbored wicked thoughts about a kind, and generous master. He was also afraid that his laziness would be exposed by the diligence of the other two servants. Most importantly, he thought it unreasonable that his labor should benefit anyone but himself. If he could have kept the profits of his labor, he might have worked hard. But working hard just to give it all to his master—what a waste of time!

The third servant represents a nominal Christian, a church-goer who technically serves God, but who has no *desire* to serve Him at all. For him, service to God is a despised duty, something to avoid as much as possible. He doesn't even invest what he has in others who will use it. He just hangs around the master's house and enjoys the pleasant atmosphere.

But salvation is not a matter of just confessing the right words and playing church. Salvation comes from faith, real faith that God is revealed in Jesus. And if God is like Jesus, then God is the most wonderful Person you've ever met. People who are truly born again have discovered in Christ the greatness of God. They see Him as the reason they exist. Serving Him is the reason they were born. Bringing Him glory is why they were made.

Biblically understood, sin is thinking you exist for your own sake, that your life is all about you, when it isn't. Faith in Christ rediscovers that we exist to fulfill our Creator's purposes. When God speaks of His people, He speaks of "everyone who is called by my name, whom I created for my glory." (Isaiah 43:7). We were made to glorify God by accomplishing His will on earth as it is in heaven.

This is great news! The world tries to find significance in how we relate to each other. "Who's on top?" The Christian finds significance in serving the One who is truly on top. We find more meaning and more joy serving at our Creator's feet on His holy mountain, living in the scope of His glory, than in standing at the top of any small mound that we cast up to glorify ourselves.

Discovering this is part of being reborn by God's Spirit. Salvation does not only involve the forgiveness of your sins. It is that, but to be spiritually reborn is also to be awakened to the glory of God. It is to exchange our old life and sense of worth for the much greater prize of living for God's glory.

That third servant obviously did not belong in the master's family. He lived among the family for awhile, but he didn't belong there. His heart was estranged from the master. He could look at the master, and not know him. He thought negative things about him, was afraid of him, didn't think him worthy of service. He was insensitive to his master's generosity and possibilities of advancement, and found no enthusiasm in contributing to his master's dreams.

The two other servants approach their master eagerly, saying "Look here! Look here! This is what you gave me. I am thrilled to give you back twice as much. I'm so pleased you trusted me with this. I don't want you to ever be sorry about entrusting me with anything, because I will use every opportunity to enrich your house. Here, take it, take it all. I count every penny's worth of labor a privilege. Give me another opportunity, and I'll do the same thing!" The master could see in those first two pairs of eyes a reflection of his own love for them. He saw in them the same devotion to the business that he had, the same devotion to his family that he had, the same devotion to him that he had for them, the same desire to make him successful that he had to share his success all around.

In the first two servants, the master found men whose hearts were after his heart. They not only earned some money, they *enjoyed* doing it for him. They enjoyed exchanging their labor for his glory. They counted it a privilege. They loved serving him; it was what they wanted to do. Rather than work for themselves and scrape together a little hovel someplace, they wanted to work for the great master and live with him, work with him, feast with him, and enjoy everything he has. The third servant could go make a living on the streets, since he didn't want to work for anyone but himself. Perhaps that describes Hell—being on your own, living forever in the poverty of your own self-centeredness, when you could have been part of the greatest project in history.

A Working Definition

This passage gives us our working definition for stewardship, the one we will be using in this study: Stewardship is finding joy in managing all God has given us for His glory. It's the attitude that my life is about God, not about me. Not that I am unimportant, mind you, but I choose to find my importance in God's importance. Instead of trying to shine with four "double A" batteries, I choose to reflect the sun.

And it is our *joy* to do so. If I cannot find joy in working hard for God, whether in cultivating my own character or raising my children or loving my neighbor or caring for the planet or building His church…if serving God is a drudgery, something I resist out of fear and selfishness…if I resent working hard so that He is glorified through my labor…then I will never do more for Him than the absolute minimum. I'll bury what He gives me, to give it back to Him one day unused. And I will never be chosen as a steward.

Stewardship understands that how I live in this age, this lifetime, is a test. All that I have been given, all the people under my care and all the stuff I have with which to care for them—as important as it is, it's all just "a few things" that God has entrusted to me in His search for managers of paradise. Every believer will be blessed to live there, but we will have differing degrees of responsibility. With whom does God wish to work most closely? Who cares about building a new creation as much as He does?

I want such a vision of God that I will work hard, work overtime. I'll get up early and stay up late. I'll use each *thing* God has entrusted to me to impact each *person* God has entrusted to me so as to bring Christ glory at His return. It doesn't matter if others have more stuff to work with, or end up influencing more people for Christ; I just want to do my very best with what God has given me. Because God is not simply looking for results; He's looking for kindred spirits.

The Lord has entrusted to our care ourselves, our families, our neighbors, this planet and His church. As tools, the Lord has given us time and money and ministry gifts. He is watching what we do with these few, small things, with His Spirit ready to help us anytime.

Christian, live for that day when the accounts are settled and your future usefulness for all eternity is determined. That day when you stand before God by grace alone, and present to Him what you've done with His investment in you. Lay your work on the table with joy. Then watch Him put aside your offering, which will suddenly seem so small in the larger scheme of things. See Him look up at you and say, "I've found a servant I want to work with. Come, share my joy as we build my dreams together!"

Prayer

Heavenly Father, we approach this matter of stewardship with humble, open hearts desiring to be filled. We confess, some of us, that we have come to see stewardship as some kind of necessary evil, or maybe a matter of paying my dues at church.

But Lord, today your Son has given us this vision of two faithful stewards, servants with very different abilities, who lit up at the opportunity to use what you invested in them to make your name a little greater in this world. Divine Master, we want to be like them. We want to be great stewards.

We know that nothing we produce will add a whole lot to your name, and it will certainly not merit our salvation. But your Son already merited our salvation, so we aren't concerned about that. We just want to use what you have entrusted to us, so that when we look over the results together, our eyes will come up from the balance sheet and see you smiling. We want that invitation to work on some really large, really glorious projects in eternity.

Hear our prayers, Father, for Jesus' sake. Amen.

Questions for Discussion

Matthew 25:14-30

What is a steward?

How is *stewardship* typically understood in a church context?

> Sometimes the subject seems a bit threatening. Why do you think that may be?

Review the parable

> Why did Jesus tell this story when He was teaching about His own future return?
>
> What in the parable suggests that these investment opportunities were a test?
>
> What was the master testing, or looking for?

Break down this definition of stewardship. Discuss and evaluate each idea:

> "Stewardship is finding joy in managing what God has given us for His glory"

Honor God with Your Body

o o o o o o o o o o o o o o o o o o o o o o o o o o o o o o o o o o

"Everything is permissible for me"—but not everything is beneficial. "Everything is permissible for me"—but I will not be mastered by anything. "Food for the stomach and the stomach for food"—but God will destroy them both. The body is not meant for sexual immorality, but for the Lord, and the Lord for the body. By his power God raised the Lord from the dead, and he will raise us also. Do you not know that your bodies are members of Christ himself? Shall I then take the members of Christ and unite them with a prostitute? Never! Do you not know that he who unites himself with a prostitute is one with her in body? For it is said, "The two will become one flesh." But he who unites himself with the Lord is one with him in spirit. Flee from sexual immorality. All other sins a man commits are outside his body, but he who sins sexually sins against his own body. Do you not know that your body is a temple of the Holy Spirit, who is in you, whom you have received from God? You are not your own; you were bought at a price. Therefore honor God with your body.

—*1 Corinthians 6:12-20*

Christian stewardship is finding joy in managing what God has given us for His glory. Salvation is a free gift, but the way we use our lives to glorify God is a test. The Lord searches for good and faithful servants among His children. What He entrusts to our care in this life are "a few things" given us to see what we think of Him, and what kind of managers we are. God is searching for stewards to whom He can entrust "many things" in eternity, partners with whom He can organize the building of a new creation for millennia to come.

God has entrusted a great deal to each of us, and the most intimate and personal trust is ourselves. Managing one person is a small test of our joy in glorifying God. So we all start with one person to manage: ourselves—our bodies and our minds.

Flesh and Blood Spirituality

The new Christians at Corinth were seriously confused about spirituality. After Paul left that city, men claiming to be "super-apostles" arrived with seductive (and lucrative) ideas about what it meant to be super-spiritual. They taught that spirituality was mainly experienced in worship services through the dramatic use of spiritual gifts. For them, following Christ was not a matter of humble ministry and trust; neither was it a matter of sacrificial love and service. They taught a spirituality of arrogance and pretense—a castle in the clouds that replaced the real power of God with emotionally charged public displays. Paul saw the radical falsehood which lay under all this junk. These harmful teachers had a view of spirituality that exalted the inner life to the exclusion of the material and the practical. One consequence was that they exalted the human spirit and disdained the human body.

However, when the Bible uses the term "spiritual," the word doesn't refer directly to the *human* spirit, but rather to *God's* Spirit. So the idea of being spiritual doesn't just deal with our spirits, but with all of life. To be spiritual is to be led by God's Spirit in every way. It involves our bodies, actions and behaviors as well as our attitudes and values. But these misguided teachers didn't see it that way. They thought that spirituality and holiness were limited to the mind and the soul, to the mental and emotional part of human nature only.

In the Corinthian letters, we see some of the ramifications that come out of a truncated, exclusively mental view of spirituality. It measured spiritual power not by deeds, but by emotionalism in worship. Their idea of spirituality did not deal with real world problems. They could have dinner together before the Lord's Supper, and not care that the poor believers among them were going hungry—they were too *spiritual* to notice! Their idea of spiritual leadership was all talk. Leaders were those who spoke well, not those who both spoke and lived well. They even expected Christ to return to take us to an ethereal, cloudlike heaven, leaving our bodies in the grave.

The notion that our bodies are insignificant is something very different from biblical Christianity. In our text, Paul reacts to some of this false teaching, such as, "Food for the stomach and the stomach for food." This saying implies that our physical nature has nothing to do with our spirituality; it is morally neutral. Physical matters don't matter in the scheme of things, so if the stomach wants food then eat what you will. The body is temporary; it doesn't matter what you do with it. Then the same argument is applied to sex, "Everything is permissible for me." Just as you feed the body when it is hungry, you give it sex when it wants sex—it doesn't matter how you do it, just do it. The body is corrupt, the body will stay in the grave forever after our spirits are freed. Therefore, any physical behavior in this life is permissible. The body has no place in salvation, so why not just do whatever feels good? On this basis, using prostitutes was justified and perhaps even encouraged in the church.

Prostitution was as common in the ancient world as it is today. Voluntary adult prostitution is legalized in the Convention on Elimination of Discrimination Against Women, a UN treaty that 165 countries have signed. President Carter signed the treaty, and it has been ratified by the Senate Foreign Relations Committee, though it has not yet passed the full Senate as of this writing. Of course, in America, prostitution *is* already legal in Nevada, and I would be surprised if more states did not follow suit. Society says, "What's the big deal? Voluntary adult sex is not a moral issue." Paul was dismayed that Christians in Corinth felt the same way, but it is a logical fall-out from the idea that spirituality is something just for the soul.

But the truth is, to be human is not to be a disembodied spirit. God created human beings as both spirit and flesh, both non-physical and physical. Salvation does not change what it means to be human. Salvation restores our humanity to God's original design. That means that salvation is about the redemption of our bodies, as well as the redemption of our souls. That's why Paul writes, "The body is not meant for sexual immorality, but for the Lord." The body is meant for the Lord, who died in the flesh to save us.

"By his power God raised the Lord from the dead, and he will raise us also." Why did God raise Jesus from the dead, if the human body is insignificant? Why didn't Jesus' spirit just go to heaven, letting His body rot? Salvation is obviously designed to save the whole person. That's why God will raise us from the grave, transforming, perfecting, and glorifying our bodies. These false teachers profoundly misunderstood what salvation is about. Salvation not only involves our spirits, but it also involves our fallen flesh and blood that will one day be glorified, transformed and destined to reflect God's character in a new creation. Therefore, our union with Christ has physical ramifications, as well as mental and emotional.

"Do you not know that your bodies are members of Christ himself?" If we are united with Christ, then all of our being is united with Christ. Not only are our spirits are united with Christ, but our bodies are also united with Christ, too. "Shall I then take the members of Christ and unite them with a prostitute? Never!" Sexual sin is not worse than other sins, but it is particularly distasteful, considering that it intimately involves our Lord.

It also involves the personal degradation of one's self. "Flee from sexual immorality. All other sins a man commits are outside his body, but he who sins sexually sins against his own body." Sexual sin assumes that a huge part of who and what I am doesn't matter to God, that nothing is holy about my body and its functions. It's like saying that a huge part of me is disposable—trash to use and throw away.

Paul says that the truth is very different. Your whole person is important, body and soul. You are in the image of God and your body is a necessary part of that image. While spirituality is rooted in the heart, it also extends to how your eyes and ears perceive the world, and how God's love flows out of your fingertips and lips. If sex is the most intimate form of physical interaction, then sex should be the *most* holy thing about us, not the least holy. False teachers proclaimed that the body is just an animal part of us; if it's hungry, feed it. Paul says, "Do you not know that your body is a temple of the Holy Spirit, who is in you, whom you have received from God?" The Holy Spirit lives in every believer. He comes alongside our spirits and dwells *within* our bodies. God the Holy Spirit is omnipresent, of course. He exists everywhere, but our bodies are His physical address on the earth. We are where He hangs His hat, where He calls "home." Believers are God's physical house.

Giving Hands and Feet to our Faith

Paul applies this in terms of stewardship. "You are not your own; you were bought at a price. Therefore honor God with your body." Christian, you and I were bought from sin at the price of Christ's blood. He bought our souls for God, so our souls belong to Him for His glory. He also bought our bodies for

God, so our bodies belong to Him, too, and must be used and managed for His glory. Using our bodies to glorify God is the first, most intimate aspect of Christian stewardship.

It seems to me that the kind of thinking that plagued Corinth is alive and well today. Many of us are tempted to restrict spiritual matters just to our thoughts and feelings. We think that we are close to God when we feel uplifted in a worship service. Certainly we want to feel uplifted in a worship service; we need that. But we are not close to God just because we feel sentimental about our religion. "He has showed you, O man, what is good. And what does the LORD require of you? To act justly and to love mercy and to walk humbly with your God." (Micah 6:8) To act justly means that we use our eyes to see injustice, our mouths to speak against it. To love mercy means that we use our feet to go to people in need, our hands to help them. "To walk humbly with our God"—the very image is a physical one of going somewhere.

James asks, "What good is it, my brothers, if a man claims to have faith but has no deeds? Can such faith save him? Suppose a brother or sister is without clothes and daily food. If one of you says to him, 'Go, I wish you well; keep warm and well fed,' but does nothing about his physical needs, what good is it? In the same way, faith by itself, if it is not accompanied by action, is dead." (James 2:14-17) The Apostle John tells us, "This is how we know what love is: Jesus Christ laid down his life for us. And we ought to lay down our lives for our brothers. If anyone has material possessions and sees his brother in need but has no pity on him, how can the love of God be in him? Dear children, let us not love with words or tongue but with actions and in truth." (1 John 3:16-18)

Truth is more than words, and love is a hands-on kind of thing. So where will we see our commitment to Christ most clearly demonstrated? *In our sexual practices*, because sex is the most intimate physical action of all. It reflects the way we honor or dishonor ourselves, other people, and our Creator, all at once. When someone refers to reproductive organs and actions as part of a curse, he proclaims part of himself to be trash. And if he thinks he is trash, then he probably feels that way about other people, too. Degrading our sexuality not only rejects God's authority, it also obscures our worth as human beings.

It is one thing to struggle with sexual temptations; everyone does. God understands our struggle, and is untiringly compassionate and patient. He never condemns anyone who yearns to live as His Word directs, even when we fail. But it's another thing to assert that what I do with my body—how I have sex, and with whom I have sex—is my business, alone. This is not biblical Christianity. Christian, when we appear before the Lord and He evaluates how well we have used what He gave us, when He examines our lives in His search for good and faithful servants, do you think it is our use of *money* that He will care about most? Or will it be how we have honored His temple?

God existed before time, without any physical thing in existence. No stars or planets, no trees or animals or angels; no light, no sound, no texture. The Lord God decided to express Himself by creating a physical universe, much the way an artist uses a physical medium to express invisible thoughts and feelings. God marked off the dimensions of the Earth, and laid its footings "while the morning stars sang together and all the angels shouted for joy." (Job 38:7) He made light and earth and sea and sky. God said, "Let us make man in our image, in our likeness, and let them rule…over all the earth." (Genesis 1:26) "The LORD God formed the man from the dust of the ground and breathed into his nostrils the breath of life, and the man became a living being." (Genesis 2:7)

Mankind was designed to be God's image in this physical world. First of all, we were granted a spirit like God's, a created part of us that transcends the physical, a part of us, like the angels, that can think and feel and plan and discern and appreciate. And then, we were given a body perfectly suited to this human spirit, a body that would enable us not only to sense and enjoy what God had made, but also to imitate Him by exercising glorious dominion over it, managing the whole thing. And we do it in families, male and female couples committed to each other, fitting together as one flesh in a way that creates yet more life, reflecting the life-giving unity and diversity of the Godhead itself. Our bodies provide the physical interface between our thoughts and desires and the physical world. They allow us to make our inner being visible, just as God did in the general creation, only on a smaller scale.

Our bodies are fundamental to the purpose for which we were made. We were not made to merely contemplate—God was not content to only contemplate. We were meant to shape and mold the physical world to express an inner spirit that thinks and feels after God's own heart. This is more than what we call "art." I'm talking about the art in everything we do and create with our senses and muscles: our homes, raising children, agriculture, industry, science—everything. We use our bodies to make our invisible values and aspirations tangible.

The fall of humanity into sin involved an inner choice that was acted out physically. The curse of sin not only impacts our feelings and intellect, but it also brought out the thorns of life that scratch and cause pain. Christ came to reverse the curse of sin, so that redeemed minds and hearts can once again imitate our Creator by shaping the material world to His glory.

If stewardship means anything, it has to involve managing the amazing, precious resource that is our body—not abusing it or treating it as something that belongs to us, to do with as our fallen natures please. "The body is...meant...for the Lord...You are not your own; you were bought at a price. Therefore honor God with your body." God is looking for stewards who find joy in bringing honor to Him by using their interface with the physical world to do wonderful things. Simple things, like lovingly brushing back the hair on your children's heads as you teach them what the world is for and what they are for, or how things are broken and how to fix them. Things more complicated, like building governments to establish justice, and economies and relief efforts that deal with human needs on a massive scale. And things most intimate, when every look and every touch communicates honor, devotion, and gratitude to share the God-given gift of life with a chosen beloved.

A Holy Temple

"Do you not know that your body is a temple of the Holy Spirit, who is in you, whom you have received from God?" The good and faithful servants whom God seeks take tremendous joy in caring for His temple. They understand that the way they treat it now reflects how they will handle and use the resurrected version forever.

For the sake of illustration, imagine that God still used a building as His Temple today, and He entrusted this building to me. How would I want to care for God's Temple, if it were a building entrusted to my care? I think I would take great satisfaction in keeping the place up. I would give the place a once over every day, pulling weeds from out front, checking for wear and tear. I would winterize it when it gets cold, and air it out in the spring. I would patch up cracks, sew up tears and replace anything eaten by termites. Of course I would—you would do the same if the Temple of the Most High were entrusted to your care. I bet we would constantly be wiping off fingerprints and sweeping up any dirt tracked in. The condition of the Temple would be a matter of honor—not just duty, but honor—an honor we would take great pleasure in.

That's how we should treat our bodies. This isn't about artificial finery, but just keeping it in good repair, good condition. Our health, our weight, our nutrition, our exercise—these are aspects of our stewardship. If only my feelings were in view, I might be content to let my body go to seed. Maybe it would not be worth it to me to spend the time and effort necessary to take care of my body. But, you see, my body does not belong to me; it is *God's* temple. God looks for servants who find joy in maintaining His temple, because they enjoy honoring Him.

I also think that if I were in charge of a Temple building, I would take great pains to see that it was used reverently, respectfully. I would allow no dangerous or profane activity on the premises—no drugs, no intoxication, no sexual immorality. That's how I should treat my body. I live with God—He *lives* in me; I'm His temple! I want Him to be able to appear at any time and not feel embarrassed about what is going on in His house. I want God to feel welcome and at home in this lodging that we share. He has certainly gone to great lengths to make me feel at home with Him.

Not only do I want to prohibit dangerous or profane activity—but I also want to make sure that it is used properly. For example, God's Temple is to be a place of worship. Worship is certainly has mental and emotional aspects, but it is also quite physical, isn't it? Worship involves using my ears and eyes to receive truth from God's written Word. Worship involves using my voice to pray to Him and sing His praises. We begin our discipleship by having our bodies washed with water. We reaffirm our discipleship by coming to a table where we commune with Him by eating and drinking together. God is looking for stewards who use their bodies for worship, lifting up holy hands in prayer, lifting up our voices with God's people to express out loud the sentiments of the heart. Believers who enjoy using their bodies for worship now, will enjoy doing so in eternity.

And, of course, God's temple is a place for outreach, a house of prayer for all people, a place any seeker could come to find God. Do you think people find God in the air, out under the stars? God's magnificent creation may, indeed, get people's attention, but people are only saved when they hear and see the gospel of Christ from another person—tangibly *hear* and *see* it. Of course, the gospel message must be understood by the mind and embraced by the heart. But Jesus said that we must tangibly show people the impact of His gospel in order to demonstrate that He is for real (John 17:20-23). We must show them in ways they can see, how we are unified in Christ, how we find our identity in Christ and have become one people in Him. That is how the world will know that He was sent from the Father. We must openly demonstrate God's love in the way we love each other. All this involves using our bodies to give God's grace a shape, a volume and mass—something people can reach out and embrace.

Christian, you have been given the responsibility to look after God's temple in this world, today. It's not a building; it's your body. Every believer has been entrusted with a body, a body originally designed "for the Lord," to express tangibly in the physical world the aspirations of God's heart. A body just as broken and corrupted by sin as our soul. A body just as redeemed as our spirit. God is looking to see which of His children enjoy managing His temple for His glory. Stewardship is about finding delight in letting God be seen, heard and felt in this world as I honor God with my body.

Prayer

We notice, Lord God, that you are a spirit. You did not need a body to make the universe, as you created all from nothing. You can simply think, and it is so. We can't do that, because we are not you. We need bodies to turn our thoughts into reality.

But we also note, Father, that you took a human body upon yourself, in the Person of your Son. You came to redeem these incredibly complex lumps of clay doomed by sin to malfunction and decay. In doing so, you demonstrated the full extent of your love. You let your body be broken for us.

After His cross, your Son was raised in glory. We wonder what will we be like when our bodies are glorified, like His? What will our loved ones who know you, look like when we see them again? Without wrinkles and stooped backs. Without glasses and false teeth. What will we look like, when our bodies are once again bursting with energy, with every sense and every member rejoicing to live for your praise?

Father, help us to be great stewards of our bodies now, in this age. Help us to show you what we think of you, through the way we use our bodies. Help us to show the world what we think of you. And with our eyes and hands and feet and lips, help us to show the world what you think of them. We pray in Jesus' name. Amen.

Questions for Discussion

1 Corinthians 6:12-20

Describe the point of view that Paul was arguing against.

Why does Paul say that sexual sin is particularly inappropriate for a believer?

Discuss the thoughts, feelings and plans you might have if you were put in charge of a physical building that God officially designated as His Temple.

Do you believe that the Holy Spirit actually lives within you?

Why or why not?
What does it mean, that the Holy Spirit lives within a Christian?

Ask for prayer concerning some way in which you wish to better honor God with your body.

The Renewing of Your Mind

o o o o o o o o o o o o o o o o o o o o o o o o o o o o o o o o o

Therefore, I urge you, brothers, in view of God's mercy, to offer your bodies as living sacrifices, holy and pleasing to God—this is your spiritual act of worship. Do not conform any longer to the pattern of this world, but be transformed by the renewing of your mind. Then you will be able to test and approve what God's will is—his good, pleasing and perfect will.

—Romans 12:1-2

Stewardship is finding joy in managing what God has given us for His glory. The most intimate form of stewardship is the management of ourselves, our bodies and our minds. This text mentions both.

The Apostle Paul begins with a reference to God's mercy. For eleven chapters, he has stressed how our Creator planned a way to conquer sinful rebels (us!) by paying for our offenses and winning our hearts. Without bending His rules or being untrue to His character, the Lord found a way to save us from misery and judgment. At this point, Paul considers how we ought to respond to such mercy. God's grace certainly deserves a response, something more than just a polite "thank you." Isaac Watts wrote that "love so amazing, so divine, demands my soul, my life, my all." The natural response to God's mercy is to offer Him ourselves unreservedly.

Paul expresses this offering as a gift of our bodies as living sacrifices, the entire tangible fruitfulness of a godly life. True worship spreads out before our eyes, like a ripple on the surface of the water—out from worship services to private and public affairs of all kinds—wider and wider and wider to encompass every conceivable phase of human endeavor. If offered to God as a living sacrifice to please Him, anything we do can be worship. Our bodies truly are temples, because they are where worship can happen 24/7, in every word, every deed, every plan, every goal—in everything!

And then, in a fashion so typical of him, Paul takes what already looks to be as large a thought as we can hold, and proceeds to expand upon it. He grasps this huge plane of activity and pulls out the whole thing into yet another dimension, giving it depth. He says that the tangible worship of our bodies is just the surface of something that goes down deep into the human soul.

This is because God always looks inside every action to see the motivations underneath. In fact, to honor God with the lips only is unacceptable; it would actually be offensive to Him. God demands that the human heart, soul, mind and emotions reflect Him, too. It's true that obedience that glorifies God cannot be real until it takes tangible shape. But it is also true that it is not real obedience unless it stems from a sincere desire within the heart. Action without the proper motivation is hypocrisy, and hypocrisy was the sin that seemed to anger Jesus the most.

God made us in His image to give concrete expression to invisible beauty. But He did not make us to be hypocrites who express a worship for Him which is not real. If we are to glorify God with the bodies He has given us, then we must at the same time glorify Him with the minds He has given us. So, the stewardship of our bodies is only half the story; the other half of personal stewardship involves our minds.

Paul says that to be good stewards of our minds, we must renew them. In one of the original *Star Trek*™ movies, Mr. Spock had problems understanding common English expressions. Once in a conversation, someone asked him if he might possibly change his mind. His response: "Is there something wrong with the one I have?" The problem with glorifying God with our mind is that something *is* wrong with the one we have. We are born with a mental and emotional predisposition to question and reject God, a predisposition that is underscored and stimulated every single day by the rebellious world around us. How can we glorify God with a spiritually damaged mind?

Paul mentions our conformity to "the pattern of this world." Intellectually and emotionally, the world is a complex place. Yet, there is a pattern that unites all of fallen mankind together: a determination to reject the authority of our Creator, and set up ourselves as the final arbiter of what is good, creating whatever gods we need in order to justify our various cultures. The pattern of this world is laced with unreasoning pride, and a greed born of hopelessness. We turn any distinction we have as a people group into a reason to think ourselves superior to others. Since the world at large has little hope beyond our few years of life on this planet, we take what we can from the Earth and from each other, with little regard for a future we do not expect to see.

Our own American version of this pattern is a bizarre, twisted Darwinian vision of reality, in which those deemed most worthy are the ones with perfect bodies and the latest technology. At its best, the American dream is about freedom and the opportunity to make something useful and worthwhile out of every life. But at its worst, it is a life-long struggle to make it to the top of the social food chain. It's a quest to have it all and experience it all at any cost, as if life were a basket of fruit to consume rather than an orchard to responsibly tend.

Our minds are trained in godless thinking from the day we are born. Sometimes by parents who have no room for God in the home. Sometimes by governmental leaders who fear the challenge of God's authority. Sometimes by educational institutions in love with their own delusions of godhood. Sometimes by economic institutions only interested in advertising themselves. How can we glorify God with a mind that thinks according to such a pattern, a pattern in which we are expected to find our glory in ourselves, in the things we possess and the flags we wave and the praise we give one another? How can a mind constantly squeezed into such a mold reflect God's character on Planet Earth? Born again minds need to be renewed.

Renewal from the Inside Out

Somewhere, thousands of miles beneath our feet, is a square meter of very dense, very hot material which is the exact center of this planet. Similarly, down deep in every soul, there is a spiritual center of gravity, a point from which all our thoughts and emotions emanate. In the Bible, this core of our inner being is most often called the *heart*. "Above all else, guard your heart, for it is the wellspring of life." (Proverbs 4:23) When we are reborn, regenerated by God's Spirit, it is this core that is miraculously brought to life, in the sense that instead of being predisposed to reject God, it is predisposed to trust Him as we were meant to.

The first evidence of new life is to embrace the simple gospel message that God will receive us back into His family and kingdom without punishment, if we will but trust His Son. From that point on, trust in the Living God begins to flow out of that wellspring of life, gradually turning sweet a soul that used to be brackish and bitter. Or to use the planetary analogy, trust in God begins to press outward, and therefore upward, from the core of our souls, gradually making its way to the surface.

Trust in God has a long way to go if it is to breach the surface of our lives and affect our behavior. Please try to imagine, if you can, how far it is from the core of this planet, to the surface. Imagine something starting at the core, trying to push and press its way to the surface, through molten metal, immense pressures and temperatures as high as 13,000 degrees. This may give us a picture of the intense struggle that Paul imagines within the human spirit, as trust in God pushes its way out from the heart through all the layers of the spirit, through all its instilled values and social pressures, to reach the surface. In order for our bodies to outwardly express godly desires in tangible ways, our mind has to be transformed, by degrees. The childlike trust implanted deep within us as a gift of the Holy Spirit must grow its way out to reshape our values and our goals and our prejudices, until finally it begins to naturally govern our behavior.

That's when God is glorified by human beings—when the whole person is involved. Remember, when it comes to stewardship, God is looking for servants who *enjoy* serving Him. The pretense of outward obedience is never enough. The joy of initially finding Christ must press through our entire mind, softening and invigorating our reasoning and our emotions. Only then will we honestly look for ways to outwardly express God's thoughts after Him.

When Paul says, "Do not conform any longer to the pattern of this world, but be transformed by the renewing of your mind," he is calling us to an active stewardship of our inner life. We are responsible to cultivate the way we think and feel, so we feel and think like God does. What a message for a society that believes that we have little control over how we feel, or how we think! God calls us to cultivate our reason and emotions, as stewards of the minds He has given us.

Godly transformation doesn't come just by fighting off old impulses. Transformation comes through the retraining and renewing of the mind. To the extent that our thoughts and our emotions are trained by faith to no longer conform to the pattern of this world, to that extent we are transformed, and we will be able to live joyful, obedient lives that glorify our God.

Picture a well. The renewing of our mind is like hauling pure trust and admiration of God all the way up from the bottom of the well, the core of our being, to soak our behavior and cause godliness to flourish. Down deep, at the heart level, the Holy Spirit regenerates us, creating sweet water underneath barren ground. Sweet water that forsakes self, forsakes sin, embraces God in Christ, rejoices in His salvation and is determined to live for Him.

But actions and behavior don't grow underground. Obedience grows on the surface of the soul, where our bodies interface with the physical world. We live life mostly by habit, and habits have shallow roots; they don't involve a lot of deep, conscious choice. For example, Christians know that God wants us to turn the other cheek when offended. Down deep, there is a pure sweetness in a reborn soul that really believes that. But when we are actually offended, we respond with our shallow rooted habits. Unfortunately, our habits have been nurtured by polluted water for many years. Ever since we first had to share a room with a sibling, we learned that the best way to defend ourselves was to give out more damage than we received, so until new habits are cultivated, that is how we naturally respond. Later, upon deeper reflection, we cringe to think how poorly we obeyed God.

There are hundreds of such examples, from racism to sex habits. On the surface of life, where we live, we are not yet convinced that God's way is the best way. Down deep, we know it is; God's Spirit has changed our hearts. But on the spur of the moment, we react with the convictions and emotions we are most familiar with, which have been nurtured by the pollution of spiritual rebellion.

Or think of it another way, since the wording "test and approve" suggests the image of ore dug from deep in the ground. When we search God's Word for truth as we would for gold, we find a fortune in raw ore. But when we are living life from moment to moment, we look at that unprocessed ore we've dug up, and it doesn't look too valuable, so we opt once again for the flashy tinsel that sparkles and catches our eye and is on sale this week, the cheap glitter everybody else is stocking up on. We choose it because we don't immediately recognize the value of God's truth.

Being transformed depends on the renewing of our mind, forming new habits of thinking that press up to where we live, forging new connections between the trust down deep in our hearts and the life we live on the surface, in our bodies, where our souls touch the world. We have to pump up that trust out of the well and cultivate obedience with it. We have to test and recognize gold in the rock we have hauled up from the mine shafts. It requires a diligent, hard working management of our faith to move truth out from the heart to fill the whole mind.

As our mind is renewed like that, look what happens, "Then you will be able to test and approve what God's will is—his good, pleasing and perfect will." There will come a time in every recurring situation when you will recognize and feel the value of God's will *before* you react. There will come a day when the water you have brought up from the well finally produces healthy fruit, and for the first time in that situation, you will glorify God by using your body—your words, looks, decisions, actions and deeds—to express His will in the real world. And you will do it not out of rote or pretense, but because you really mean it. Your obedience will be honest and joyful because your mind is renewed to appreciate His will.

The Work of Renewal

Obviously, the renewing of our minds doesn't just happen automatically. The verbs here are imperative verbs, they call us to action. They call us to continuous action, to a lifestyle of stewardship, in fact. How will you and I ever hope to exercise good stewardship over our families, relationships, environment and God's church, let alone over mere tools such as time and money, if we are not first of all stewards of our minds? Offering our lives as tangible, living sacrifices of worship depends on being transformed by the renewing of our minds. How do we find such transformation?

Surely the answer lies in two directions. On the one hand, we must counter or resist conformity with the world's pattern of thinking. On the other hand, we must cultivate God's thoughts and emotions as they are all perfectly revealed in Christ, who is perfectly revealed in the Scriptures. Let's look at several areas involved in renewing our minds: education, meditation, media and fellowship.

Education is so important because of the power of authority figures. To be educated means that you put yourself under someone else to be taught. You allow your thinking to be shaped by others, by the instructors you choose and the materials they use. You are molded by the philosophy and curriculum and educational goals of your teachers.

A single comment by an authority figure can burn itself into your brain and become a principle you use to guide your whole life—how much more the repeated declarations and implications impressed upon you by your teachers over and over and over again throughout your schooling! Endure public embarrassment just once from a teacher because of your biblical beliefs, and you might carry a false sense of shame with you throughout your school years. By the same token, a teacher can confirm your biblical faith just as easily and profoundly. Choosing the people who will teach you is one of the most important stewardship decisions you will ever make concerning yourself.

As a pastor, I am aware, week after week, that the church is the prime instrument of education for God's people. Pastors and other church leaders will answer to God for what we teach, because pastoring is a special stewardship. But even in the church, you are also responsible for the stewardship of your mind. To begin with, choosing a church home is an exercise of your stewardship. I'm not talking about the investment of your money; I'm talking about the investment of your mind. The pastors and churches you choose are exercises of your personal stewardship.

And if that is true, then what about the other educational authorities you choose for yourself? Like which college you attend? Like which books you read, and what commentators you follow on radio and TV? You are responsible for what and who you allow to shape your thinking. You can, and should, study from many sources in order to understand other points of view, but you must choose which voices you *listen* to, to guide your thinking. Every "expert" does not carry equal weight with God. We must give thought to the godliness, biblical knowledge and character of the voices we choose to educate and inform us. Why learn our pattern of thinking from people who neither know the Living God nor care to know Him? Educational choices are part of the stewardship of our mind.

Another way to renew the mind is through *meditation*. Christian meditation (as opposed to Eastern meditation) is an attempt to learn from the Holy Spirit Himself as our teacher. With education, I place myself under another human mentor, trusting God's Spirit to guide him or her. With meditation, I try to experience the Holy Spirit as my Mentor more directly. The Holy Spirit does this by enlightening our minds to His written revelation.

As stewards of the minds God gave us, we must learn to meditate. Learn to examine Scripture verses in context, considering whole biblical themes from all sides. Meditation is about learning new things from God's Word every time you look at it, or better appreciating things you already know. Ask questions of a verse or a text and ask the Holy Spirit to give you insight. Consider one word at a time and ask how that particular biblical word makes a difference. Let the Holy Spirit use the Scriptures to teach you how to think.

And also learn to feel with the Holy Spirit as your teacher. Learn to grieve as sin grieves Him, and to sing along as righteousness and mercy move Him to song. Meditation is about learning how to weep properly and how to rejoice properly.

Learn to explain, summarize and paraphrase the Bible to the Holy Spirit, so He can bounce it back to you so as to correct and perfect your understanding. You can get a real dialog going with Him. Let your passion build until you ask, "What are we going to do about this?"

Devote time to meditation. Use whatever techniques will work for you. I've turned my half hour of daily exercise into a min-retreat by using music. I choose music that stimulates godly emotions within me, music that makes me feel grateful to be alive, willing to serve and strive and sacrifice alongside my Lord, music that stirs my highest aspirations. At the same time, I fantasize about doing things that delight Him. I practice them in my mind, so that when real opportunities actually come for service, I'll be just a little more ready to respond so as to please His heart. I'm trying to stir up the beliefs and passions of my heart all the way to the surface, until my soul swells with pride in my Lord and I weep tears of joy.

I also like to play with ideas, so I use children's blocks, associating a biblical theme with each block as I build a simple structure. I also enjoy reflecting upon God's greatness as I gaze into the sky, as well as spending quiet moments with Him discussing His will, using a room of the house especially set aside for prayer.

You find your own techniques. Find things that work for you so you can study God's Word at the feet of the Holy Spirit.

In terms of day to day practicality, few things influence the mind more than the modern *media*. Entertainment, news and games have a very large potential to shape how we think, either to conform us into the world's pattern of thinking, or enhance our renewal in the Holy Spirit.

Paul instructed, "whatever is true, whatever is noble, whatever is right, whatever is pure, whatever is lovely, whatever is admirable—if anything is excellent or praiseworthy—think about such things." (Philippians 4:8) However, contemporary media is so commanding and intrusive that it is likely to override any conscious attempt to focus the mind as Paul mentioned. Video, music and computer games are highly persuasive, intimidating, seductive and repetitive. Therefore, it is important to thoughtfully choose and handle media sources.

The first step is to make sure we have the self-control to personally censure the media we use. Images, dramatic scenes and music cannot be easily erased from the mind. To a large extent, what goes in, stays in. We like to think that we are mature enough to handle some distasteful material. Of course we are. But if something is of no use at all in renewing my mind, why do I want it tattooed on my soul? We want to benefit from all the good material out there, but we must be prepared to shut down, turn off or walk out on whatever is not worth the effort to filter.

However, while some things should be shut out entirely, the key is to learn to filter media effectively. Rather than hide from everything, we want to sample what is available. To do so safely, we need to compare everything we see or hear against Paul's criteria of truth, nobility, purity, beauty and excellence. "Test everything. Hold on to the good." (1 Thessalonians 5:21) Authors, producers and performers want us to suspend disbelief and take us in a ride through their minds. We need to practice remaining objective, identifying and mentally labeling that which falls short of biblical standards. A great way to practice this is to discuss what we have just seen or heard with others.

When we have marked off dangerous territory to filter out, we can then profit from the rides of perception and imagination media can provide. Being firmly grounded in the truth does not mean we have to be stuck in the mud. Christians should excel in using their creativity and sensitivity. Good media sources can stimulate that.

That is why Christians need to rediscover how to patronize the arts and promote the production of excellent material. In particular, we need to learn how to bring a biblical worldview to non-religious themes in drama, writing and music. Traditionally, evangelical Christians have all but abandoned professional artistic pursuits, especially in the movie industry. Our minds will be greatly enriched as we could rediscover our voice in these areas.

Christian *fellowship* is also an important part of the renewing of our minds. Good fellowship reminds me of a property of sound called resonance. When sound waves resonate, they bounce back upon themselves in such a way as to accumulate and amplify their energy. My most memorable experience of this was in Israel, in an old Crusader church. Its stone walls were perfectly spaced to amplify the human voice. That building convincingly demonstrated to me the ancient church's preference for choral singing over preaching. Musical tones seemed to ring through the space forever. On the other hand, every spoken word reverberated and echoed so persistently that it was impossible to complete a sentence!

Fellowship acts to resonate our faith. The small song of trust murmuring down deep in our heart echoes off of others. Fellowship bounces the truth back and forth, accumulating energy. Wisdom and understanding multiply, along with passion and zeal. We experience new aspects of faith vicariously, through fellow believers, so we are better prepared for challenges we have yet to face. The energy of our faith builds and more quickly fills the whole mind.

Seek out godly fellowship. Seek out brothers and sisters with whom you can talk about your faith, your struggles, your victories, your new insights and your new questions. Find people you like to sit next to in church, so you can sing together. If fellowship is such a powerful influence in renewing our minds, then it must be part of our stewardship, too.

Stewardship is finding joy in managing the mind God has given me for His glory. When you stand before God and offer everything you produced for Him, do you really think that His first concern will be your bank account? He's looking for stewards to whom He can entrust His vision of paradise. Imagine how excitedly He will look for what you have done with the fantastic mind He gave you, the one the world tried so hard to bend to its collective will. "What did you do to bring to the surface all the wonderful things my Spirit brought you?" What will He find when He looks at your mind, at the thoughts and feelings you cultivated so as to motivate how you actually live? Will He be disappointed? If so, He would love you none the less; Christ's redemption is perfect. But He could be disappointed at our lack of effort.

Or, He could see a mind that has already been faithfully renewed in thought and emotion, a mind capable of inspiring the joyful obedience of the body, which is our worship. "I see that you have enjoyed thinking my thoughts after me. There are so many more ideas in my mind! How would you like to work with me to bring them into reality?"

Prayer

Heavenly Father, your Holy Spirit planted the seed of faith within us. At the core of our being, we trust you. Because of Jesus, we trust you. But we need to haul that living water up from a deep, deep well to moisten the habits of thinking and feeling that grow on the surface of our lives. O Lord, help us. Help us to renew our minds.

You have already sent us a Helper. Your Holy Spirit lives within our bodies like a temple. We want Him to be our teacher. We want to learn from Him as we meditate on your Word, study with other godly teachers, fill our minds with helpful images, and sharpen our thoughts with other brothers and sisters.

Father, transform us by the renewing of our minds, so we can recognize and joyfully embrace your good and perfect will. We pray in Jesus' name. Amen.

Questions for Discussion

Romans 12:1-2

What does it mean to be "conformed to the pattern of this world"?

What's wrong with this world's pattern?
What forces tend to conform us to it?

Why does our mind need to be renewed? What's wrong with it?

How does the Holy Spirit "renew the mind"? (see Titus 3:5-7, where the same word for "renewal" is used)

Discuss how our mental renewal can be helped or hindered by:

Education
Meditation
Media
Fellowship

Watching Over the Affairs of the Household

o o o o o o o o o o o o o o o o o o o o o o o o o o o o o o o o o

The sayings of King Lemuel—an oracle his mother taught him: "O my son, O son of my womb, O son of my vows, do not spend your strength on women, your vigor on those who ruin kings. "It is not for kings, O Lemuel—not for kings to drink wine, not for rulers to crave beer, lest they drink and forget what the law decrees, and deprive all the oppressed of their rights. Give beer to those who are perishing, wine to those who are in anguish; let them drink and forget their poverty and remember their misery no more.

"Speak up for those who cannot speak for themselves, for the rights of all who are destitute. Speak up and judge fairly; defend the rights of the poor and needy."

A wife of noble character who can find? She is worth far more than rubies. Her husband has full confidence in her and lacks nothing of value. She brings him good, not harm, all the days of her life. She selects wool and flax and works with eager hands. She is like the merchant ships, bringing her food from afar. She gets up while it is still dark; she provides food for her family and portions for her servant girls. She considers a field and buys it; out of her earnings she plants a vineyard. She sets about her work vigorously; her arms are strong for her tasks. She sees that her trading is profitable, and her lamp does not go out at night. In her hand she holds the distaff and grasps the spindle with her fingers. She opens her arms to the poor and extends her hands to the needy. When it snows, she has no fear for her household; for all of them are clothed in scarlet. She makes coverings for her bed; she is clothed in fine linen and purple. Her husband is respected at the city gate, where he takes his seat among the elders of the land. She makes linen garments and sells them, and supplies the merchants with sashes. She is clothed with strength and dignity; she can laugh at the days to come. She speaks with wisdom, and faithful instruction is on her tongue. She watches over the affairs of her household and does not eat the bread of idleness. Her children arise and call her blessed; her husband also, and he praises her: "Many women do noble things, but you surpass them all." Charm is deceptive, and beauty is fleeting; but a woman who fears the LORD is to be praised. Give her the reward she has earned, and let her works bring her praise at the city gate.

—Proverbs 31

Stewardship is finding joy in managing what God has given us for His glory. The way we manage what God has entrusted to us in this life enables our Lord to evaluate our faithfulness and joy as His steward. He is looking for people to administer a new Earth, a new creation, at Christ's return. Our stewardship today reveals those he wants in leadership tomorrow. Stewardship begins with ourselves, with our own bodies and minds.

But stewardship includes more than just ourselves. It includes our children, as well. By "our children," I really mean the next generation. When Adam and Eve were sentenced to death for their sin, that sentence was partially suspended to allow them to live long enough to bear children and keep the race alive. That way, all the human beings God had destined for life would be born. Ever since, one of the principal responsibilities of every generation has been to bear and prepare the next generation.

In particular, one of the responsibilities belonging to every generation of the church is to prepare the next generation of the church. Besides our stewardship of the gospel to the unchurched, we have a stewardship of the children God entrusts to us. This is a stewardship that everyone in the church shares. Couples, singles, single parents, we all work together as a church family, both formally in various programs and informally as we help each other raise the kids God has entrusted to us. The Bible teaches us to treat our children as disciples of Christ, baptizing them and teaching them to obey all He has commanded. This is a crucial part of our stewardship.

I've chosen a fairly familiar text, but I am going to approach it a little differently than you might expect. You may have heard of "the Proverbs 31 woman," the biblical description of a good wife. Our text is the entire chapter that contains that description, but we won't be focusing on the role of a woman in the home. In Proverbs 31, King Lemuel applies what he learned about a godly home to the role of the mother. Had he applied it to a godly father, he might have illustrated the principles with different specific duties, but I believe the areas covered would be exactly the same. Our goal in this study is to consider what a godly home looks like, rather than just a godly wife and mother. As stewards of the children God has entrusted to us, let's look to this text to see what kind of people He expects our training to produce.

Life Skills

King Lemuel may have been one of the great wise men of the region drawn to Solomon and Solomon's God. His name means *belonging to God*, suggesting that his mother had come to faith first. In fact, the way this chapter is structured, the section concerning the home is an intricate poem following the wisdom given Lemuel by his mother. Each verse begins with a different letter of the Hebrew alphabet. It forms a verbal picture of the virtuous wife and mother, in contrast to the kind of woman mentioned in first few verses, who is drawn to the abuse of power. This poem is included here to emphasize the extraordinary value of a good, stable home. The influential, rich and famous could, and often do, lose themselves in power, sex and drugs (all of which are mentioned in the first section of the chapter). But in the end, a well-functioning home is of far greater worth.

There are skills that make life stable and reasonably happy. These skills are different from gimmicks that obtain perverse pleasure cheaply. Lemuel's mother speaks of "forgetting what the law decrees, and depriving all the oppressed of their rights." Anyone who has any power, from a Cabinet position to supervising one other employee on the night shift, can learn to derive perverse pleasure from controlling others. Proverbs 31 also speaks of alcohol intoxicating the mind, whether in pursuit of the eternal party, or in search of self-medicated relief. That's another twisted pleasure one can become very good at. The text says the same thing about sex. Sex divorced from friendship and commitment, "loving" people you haven't really learned to even like, is another bitter art people develop.

In contrast to these worthless shortcuts are true life skills, skills to live in a way that is fundamentally healthy. These skills do not produce the kicks of common perversities, but neither do they produce the bruises. The skills practiced and taught and learned in a good home bring happiness and stability over the long haul. They keep people relatively whole and healthy, both physically and emotionally. They keep a society relatively whole and healthy, too. Without them, individuals, even entire cultures, may flash brightly for a time, but they inevitably burn out. These life skills must be passed on from stable adults in order to train stable children.

For example, there are the very basic skills involved in taking care of oneself and one's family. "She is like the merchant ships, bringing her food from afar. She gets up while it is still dark; she provides food for her family and portions for her servant girls. When it snows, she has no fear for her household; for all of them are clothed in scarlet. She makes coverings for her bed; she is clothed in fine linen and purple." Thoughtfully designed and well made clothing adorns the body just as tasteful furnishings adorn a living space. Both communicate self respect and therefore command the respect of others. Notice the special emphasis placed on nutrition. The woman in question does not simply pick up what is fast and easy at the market. She is like a merchant ship, carefully selecting a variety of food brought in from some distance to feed her family intelligently and well. People do not physically take care of themselves very well, by nature; it is a skill that must be learned.

On top of that are the skills needed to financially prosper. Look at all the references to economics in this poem: "She considers a field and buys it; out of her earnings she plants a vineyard." "She sees that her trading is profitable, and her lamp does not go out at night." "She makes linen garments and sells them, and supplies the merchants with sashes." Did you know that the word *economics* comes from the Greek word for *household*? Not only is the family designed to be the bedrock of a nation's prosperity, but prosperity is something that has to be learned in the home. The value of money, recognizing good opportunities from foolish ones, commitment to a job and a career, being satisfied with an honest profit, producing something of value—these skills have kept people from poverty and want for centuries. No one is born knowing them; they must be learned and practiced.

And with prosperity comes social responsibility. "She opens her arms to the poor and extends her hands to the needy." This picks up on a quote Lemuel remembers from his own mother, "Speak up for those who cannot speak for themselves, for the rights of all who are destitute. Speak up and judge fairly; defend the rights of the poor and needy." Every human being has a responsibility to other human beings in need. If we are to do to others as we wish them to do for us, then we must certainly reach out to the poor and to the needy. And not only *to* the needy, but also *for* them—represent them to their advantage, since they cannot usually represent themselves very well. Responsibility for others who suffer poverty and oppression does not come naturally. The poor feel disenfranchised, the rich feel too threatened, the middle class is too distracted. At every social level, caring for people in need is a life skill, a discipline that must be taught and learned.

And then, there are all those critical skills involved in cultivating positive relationships. Lemuel stresses the relationships that fill a healthy home, "A wife of noble character…is worth far more than rubies. Her husband has full confidence in her…She brings him good, not harm, all the days of her life." "Her children arise and call her blessed; her husband also, and he praises her: 'Many women do noble things, but you surpass them all.'" Strong, positive relationships do not just happen; they have to be built, built from the ground up and constantly maintained. In a godly home, the wife concentrates on bringing her husband good, not harm—not once in a while, not when she feels like it, but "all the days of her life." The poem itself is a lovingly crafted praise of a husband for his wife. She is worth more than rubies, he has full confidence in her and he leads the children in singing her praises as the best of the best. Many skills must be learned in order to build these kinds of positive relationships, including the self-control to maintain consistent good will, kindness, thoughtfulness, and patience, as well as the commitment to resolve conflicts in a way that helps and heals all parties. These skills do not come naturally or automatically; they must be learned and they must be practiced.

And perhaps all the other skills depend on a strong inner character. "She is clothed with strength and dignity." This woman has a sterling reputation for hard work. "She selects wool and flax and works with eager hands." "She sets about her work vigorously; her arms are strong for her tasks." "In her hand she holds the distaff and grasps the spindle with her fingers." She gets up before dawn and works until after dark. When strong character is recognized, we call it a *reputation.* "Give her the reward she has earned, and let her works bring her praise at the city gate." "Her husband is respected at the city gate, where he takes his seat among the elders of the land." Consistent diligence brings dignity, the recognition of an inner strength of character. A capacity for hard work is not natural; it has to be trained.

These are "the affairs of the household." They are what every generation must pass on to the next generation. As Christians, we recognize them as part of our stewardship of the children God has entrusted to us.

Failing the Next Generation

You can relate so much of the social deterioration of our nation to our general unwillingness to practice these skills and teach them to our children. Children are not learning the basic skills of how to live well, how to live successfully. Perhaps today's parents, by and large, did not learn them well from their parents, and the breakdown has been getting worse over each successive generation for a while now. At this point, the rising generation is losing its grip even on the basic skills of caring for themselves. A hot topic these days is obesity in children. Obesity in the general population is discouraging, but it is the trends in our children which are the most alarming, and perhaps the most revealing about our failure to pass along life skills.

The number of obese children has doubled over the last 20 years. Children who eat fast food every day (almost a third of all US children) gain an extra 6 pounds a year. This is combined with an increasingly sedentary lifestyle. The implications for diabetes, heart disease, high blood pressure, mobility limitations and stroke are serious, not to mention the emotional challenges of living in a world that worships "thin." Many young people don't know how to shop for food, prepare it, or eat well when dining out. And nutrition is just one of the life skills needed to take care of oneself.

How well do our young people understand sound economics? Of course, homes accustomed to poverty are ill equipped to prepare their children to prosper. But it is the upper middle class that struggles today to pass on a sense of the value of money and a commitment to produce something of value for society. What about the most basic principles of money management? How many children leave home already using a personal budget? What about savings? tithing? Do they understand how to use and not use credit, how to intelligently shop or buy a car?

And assuming they find prosperity, do our children link it with their responsibilities to their fellow man? Lemuel could still quote his mother's words about speaking out for those who can't speak for themselves. I wonder what children today are able to quote from their parents? Do they remember their Mom and Dad telling them to care for refugees, or help people in the inner city turn their life around, if they are willing to do so? What's going to happen to Baby Boomers when the poor and disenfranchised are *us* in old age, and our children are faced with the responsibility to care for us? Will they have learned from us compassion and responsibility for the weak?

Clearly the rising generations knows less and less about building stable relationships. Trends in the home do not bode well for learning relationship building skills. Careers keep many parents from having much time *living* with their children. In 1995, 4 of 5 families saw TV as a family experience. Today, more than half of the children in the US have a TV in their own rooms. This is not to mention a growing number of computers, which take up an hour or more of time every day, and also tend to be used privately, making the home a still more isolated place. The interaction that comes from just living together—baking, gardening, working on house projects or automobile maintenance, even flying a kite—all the opportunities to share the memories and experiences of parents and grandparents are being lost.

On top of this, so many of our families feel isolated because they are broken. Divorce teaches children that real relationships just can't hold up under the stress of life. They learn to distrust marriage, or deal with problems the way they saw their own parents deal with them—by breaking up. They learn that men and women cannot live together; their understanding of marriage and sexual relationships becomes bruised, even warped. That's not what we want to teach them, but it's what they learn.

And the lack of stable relationships has a profound impact on a child's inner character. The loose sex and addictive drugs and abuse of power that Lemuel had to deal with haven't gone away. If anything, we have a much wider selection of them now. The details of addiction may change (even video games have been shown to release dopamine in the brain), but they always eat away at our inner integrity.

We put so much stress today on teaching a positive self image, but it is difficult to have a sense of personal dignity without an ingrained commitment to hard work, the willingness to do what needs doing. Children need dignity, simple self respect based on a capacity for honest, hard work that takes care of the details of life and does not expect those details to magically take care of themselves. These are the life skills that help define the stewardship of our children.

Our society does not think of children as a stewardship. We tend to get married purely for personal convenience; there is rarely today any sense of a covenant with God to honor Him and raise the next generation to His glory. And when children happen (and we allow them to be born), they are not precious responsibilities entrusted to us by God. They are our possessions, to mold in whatever way we find convenient and satisfying.

Serious Christians, of course, think otherwise. We never consider another human being as belonging to us like a possession. We see children as gifts of grace entrusted to our care for a short time. We dedicate them to God and work hard to raise them accordingly. After all, "Charm is deceptive, and beauty is fleeting; but a woman who fears the LORD is to be praised." To fear God is to take Him and His design for life seriously—more seriously than anything else. Without God, all the world has left is charm and beauty, brief resources, at best, and often deceptive. Faith in God supports everything else. Born again Christians work very hard to teach their children religious truths. We bring them to excellent Sunday Schools. We read them Bible stories and pray with them, perhaps even teach them the Catechism. We want our children to know the gospel; we want them to know our Savior.

Building on a Religious Foundation

That is excellent as far as it goes. But I think this text in Proverbs challenges contemporary Christians who see the stewardship of their children in exclusively religious terms. We need to rediscover that fearing God is much more than religious instruction. Godly religion is the foundation upon which life can be built, but the life skills we need to live successfully have to actually be built on that foundation. They don't just develop all by themselves.

Fearing God means to take Him seriously in *all* of life. Proverbs 31 says of the godly parent, "She speaks with wisdom, and faithful instruction is on her tongue." Certainly that instruction begins with the covenant of salvation, but it goes on from there. The very next verse asserts, "She watches over the affairs of her household." The affairs of a household involve the life skills of taking care of yourself, prospering economically, caring for the poor and disenfranchised, building successful, positive, stable relationships. All this is based on a sense of dignity before the Living God, whom we serve by doing whatever needs to be done to carry out His will.

What Lemuel called "fearing God"—which we now know as Christian discipleship—requires these basic life skills. Discipleship is not only about Bible study and prayer. Presumably our prayer and Bible study will call us to live differently, and live *better*. But how can we live better if we don't have the dignity to do what needs to be done in order to follow our Lord? How can we develop the dignity to do what needs to be done without stable relationships with people who will be there for us, and encourage us, just as we do for them? How can our relationships be honest and without hypocrisy if we will not responsibly care for people just like us, except that they are poor and oppressed and in need? How can we help such people, let alone finance God's church, if we have never learned how to financially prosper? How can we hope to financially prosper, if we can't even take care of our own personal health and hygiene?

Our society has been deteriorating in terms of its life skills over several generations. While some of us have had great parental training and have found good success in passing these skills on to our kids, many of us have not. It's hard to pass on what you never received yourself. But if we don't do a better job with the stewardship of our children, they will be in an even worse position when raising *their* kids for God. And if that happens, the future church will be weakened because of our poor stewardship.

Christian, let's ask God to enable us to turn this trend around. By God's grace, let's go beyond ourselves in our stewardship of the next generation. Let's give them a better stewardship than we ever received ourselves. Isn't that the goal of every good parent, to give their children more than they ever had? God will help us. "I can do everything through him who gives me strength." (Philippians 4:13) Let's give our children more and better life skills than we ever received growing up. Let's teach them how to take care of themselves. Let's teach them how to earn a living, and save and invest and prosper. Let's teach them a commitment to use their prosperity to help those who cannot prosper through no fault of their own. Let's teach them how to build relationships that are positive and that will last.

Let's teach them the kind of dignity that isn't afraid to work hard to become all God has called them to be.

We probably can't do this all by ourselves. We are going to have to help each other. Some of us are going to have to do some make-up work to master some of these skills ourselves, before we can teach them to our children. It's hard work, but I believe God will give us the dignity to accomplish it.

One day, He will look over our stewardship of the generation that followed us. He'll receive our imperfect labors with love, perfect love bought and secured by the blood of Christ. But He'll also be looking for people who faithfully raised the children entrusted to them—the children in their home, church, and community. He'll be looking for good stewards who will love and care for the rest of His beloved children for ages and ages to come. And there will be some of us whom He will call forward, saying: "You were faithful with the few children I entrusted to you. Come, I have a rather large family I want you to help look after..."

Prayer

Father, we call you "Father" because we are your children through Christ, your only beloved Son. And you have called us to be fathers and mothers and grandparents and aunts and uncles and older brothers and sisters to a particular group of children coming up after us. You have entrusted them to our care, just as you entrusted us to the generation before us.

We thank you for our parents and all the others of their generation who have helped us become the people we are—who gave us, in some measure, the life skills we needed to take your revealed will for our lives and put it into practice. We especially see their influence in the most mature among us.

Now, Heavenly Father, we recognize that it is our turn. We are doing our best to teach the children you have given us how to know your Son, how to understand your Word, and how to pray. Father, help us to also build on that foundation, and teach them how to live—live in a way that honors your design for life.

Father, some of us are embracing this part of our stewardship a bit late. We wish we could go back and do some things differently. But you would not have us dwell on what is past, but rather look forward to what you can still do through us. So Father, help us to enable our children to effectively live for you in their generation, so they can then pass on those skills to their children, until the day your Son returns and the redeemed of every generation get about the business of life in earnest. Hear us, we pray, in Jesus' name. Amen.

Questions for Discussion

Proverbs 31

Does our society see children in terms of stewardship?

If not, how does our society view children?

Discuss the sorts of things people need to learn today in order to...

Take care of their own health and hygiene
Earn and manage money well
Take care of the poor and needy
Establish and maintain healthy relationships
Develop a strong work ethic

Which of the above skills can we expect our children to learn well at church? at school?

How can we be sure to teach the rest of them at home? What do we need to do?
If we are weak in some of these skills ourselves, what can we do to learn them?

He Who Loves His Fellowman
Has Fulfilled the Law

o o o o o o o o o o o o o o o o o o o o o o o o o o o o o o o o o o

Let no debt remain outstanding, except the continuing debt to love one another, for he who loves his fellowman has fulfilled the law. The commandments, "Do not commit adultery," "Do not murder," "Do not steal," "Do not covet," and whatever other commandment there may be, are summed up in this one rule: "Love your neighbor as yourself." Love does no harm to its neighbor. Therefore love is the fulfillment of the law.

—*Romans 13:8-10*

Stewardship is finding joy in managing what God has entrusted to me for His glory. The Lord loves all His children equally because He loves us perfectly in Christ. But at the final judgment, He will be looking for those who have proven themselves to be faithful stewards in this life, believers who really *enjoy* serving Him. He wants them to take the lead in building His eternal kingdom.

Beyond managing our own bodies and minds, stewardship broadens out to include other people, beginning with the family and, in particular, the children He entrusts to us. Our stewardship of people does not end there, however. It also includes people who are not part of our family, people who can be described by the generic term "neighbor." Indeed, our stewardship of people may be much broader and far more exciting than we may have expected.

An Ongoing Debt

"Let no debt remain outstanding, except the continuing debt to love one another." Every responsible adult is committed to pay his or her debts. Whether the debt is one of taxes to the government, or the minimum payment on a credit card bill, or the mortgage, or a car payment. Paul said that Christians take such responsibilities seriously for two reasons. First, just like everyone else, we fear the repercussions of not doing so. Second, our consciences insist that we fulfill our obligations. Every obligation we have to another human is considered binding by our God. Therefore, every valid human obligation is also an obligation to our Lord.

In the Psalms, King David made the same point, that no matter who else we offend, every sin is a sin against God (Psalm 51:1-4). Paul turns that around; every obligation we fulfill is an act of faithfulness toward God. In our text, Paul expands that idea out to its broadest possible application. There is one debt that is always outstanding, always due and as ongoing as our worship: our never ending obligation to love each other.

It's important to remember that the kind of love mentioned here (*agape* in the Greek) is neither a matter of romance nor of family obligation. *Agape* love is simple, honest good will toward another person. It imitates God's love. It reflects a sincere commitment to another person's well being, quite independent of our relationship with that person or what he/she thinks of us. *Agape* love is not created by circumstances or drawn out by the person loved; it flows out of an overflowing heart. From God, it flows out of His essential, pure goodness. From us, it flows out of our gratitude for God's grace.

Because of the undeserved mercy God has given us in Christ, every Christian is obligated to honor God by extending honest good will and mercy to others. This is a debt that we owe. Ultimately, it is a debt that we owe to God, but practically, it is a debt we pay by caring for others. There are no boundaries around this debt. God's mercy is comprehensive. We therefore owe a debt of love involving our entire lives, and we owe this debt to every human being we come across.

Paul explains love for everyone as an ongoing obligation by putting it in biblical terms. "Let no debt remain outstanding, except the continuing debt to love one another, for he who loves his fellowman has fulfilled the law." In the Old Testament, God created an external reflection of the internal heart He is constructing within His chosen, covenant people. This is called the "Law." The Law was more than rules; it included examples and stories and principles, as well. It was most classically summarized in 10 Commandments. Paul lists some of the commandments that deal with human relationships. "Do not commit adultery," "Do not murder," "Do not steal," "Do not covet." Then Paul quotes the teaching of Jesus that all such commandments are summarized by one principle, one "golden rule" from Leviticus: "Love your neighbor as yourself." Paul's summary explanation is very simple; "Love does no harm to its neighbor. Therefore love is the fulfillment of the law."

The Holy Spirit imprints the Law of God on the heart of every new believer (2 Corinthians 3:3-6). An honest desire to do good to other people is the increasingly natural response of anyone who has truly embraced the love of God in Jesus Christ. "Christ's love compels us, because we are convinced that one died for all, and therefore...those who live [through Him] should no longer live for themselves." (2 Corinthians 5:14-15) Christians have a sense of inner obligation to treat others kindly and mercifully, regardless of who they are, what they are, or what they've done. None of that matters when it comes to what we owe them, because God was willing to treat us mercifully and kindly in Christ, regardless of what we owed Him.

This compulsion to love is not all that we feel toward people, of course. It competes with all the old self-centered habits that ruined us in the first place. But it is a new component of our being, one that grows as our spirit gets healthier. And this inner attitude of honest good will naturally fulfills any godly law ever written. Remember, the written law was given to reflect the inner soul the God requires and cultivates within His children. So, to the extent that the Holy Spirit cultivates a loving soul within us, to that extent we naturally fulfill God's holy law without even thinking about it.

If loving our fellowman is an obligation upon all Christians, then the people we have opportunity to love must be included in our stewardship. Remember that in the ancient world, stewards were not only in charge of things, but they were also often in charge of caring for people. Our Romans text doesn't seem to refer just to that small number of people whom we call our own family. Neither is it limited to that much larger group of people called the church, with whom we share a common faith and a future in paradise. It is wide open, including all the other people who are alive at the same time we are. People just like us socially, but who are strangers to us. People who are not like us socially. People who are not like us ethnically, or nationally. We are obligated to love all people; we acknowledge our debt to God by doing them good from an honest good will.

No Artificial Boundaries

"Love your neighbor as yourself." Loving our fellowman in this broadest context is a part of our Christian stewardship. It is a daily aspect of our stewardship which has no artificial limits. This usually raises the question of boundaries. What are the boundaries of my stewardship to my fellowman? I can't meet all the needs of all the world. This was the concern of a biblical scholar who debated with Jesus, as recorded in Luke 10. It seemed clear to this scholar that God's command to love your neighbor as yourself had to imply some kind of limitation. As the parable of the Good Samaritan showed him, the problem comes when we try to establish artificial boundaries. When he asked, "Who is my neighbor?" he wanted some way to restrict the people he was responsible to love, or care about. From a biblical perspective, this is very wrong-headed thinking, motivated by guilt. We see a homeless person on the highway, and feel guilty about passing him by. We see pictures of starving or diseased individuals, and turn away; we want to somehow eliminate them from our responsibility because we feel guilty about not being able to help all such people.

God never wants His people to turn anyone away because we feel guilty. That's a futile attempt to define who our neighbor is, in such a way as to exclude somebody. "I can't feed the whole world, so I'll pretend that it isn't my responsibility to feed anybody." Jesus forbade us from defining anyone as a "non-neighbor," to whom we owe nothing. We are to be neighbors to all people.

Of course, we cannot meet everyone's needs. God has limited our resources, and the Bible makes it clear that we are only responsible for the resources we have, not for resources we don't have. (2 Corinthians 8:12) Most of our resources are already committed, by God's design, to take care of the specific responsibilities of our family, our church and taxes. God does not expect us to help everyone. Jesus simply wants us to put no *artificial* limitations on our obligation to do good to other people.

We never have all that we want, or as much as somebody else. But God gives us what we need, and usually more, so we can share. In fact, we almost always have more than we need, if we are willing to sacrifice a little. Think of the widow who gave two pennies at the Temple (Luke 21:1-4). Jesus said it was all that she had. That is, she gave her food money for the day. She chose to give to the Temple rather than eat. On that day, she might have thought she had nothing to give, but then realized that if she fasted, she could give something. Not much, but something. She left the Temple with the joy of giving, not feeling poor, but rich. The people who are truly poor are those who have nothing to give. Whether it be money, time or energy, they are so poor that they have nothing to spare. Many of the world's richest, most healthy and most energetic are too poor to help another human being. And many of the world's least healthy and wealthy are much richer because they always have something to share.

So, how poor are you? How poor am I? Am I so poor that I live in guilt and fear, with nothing to share with those in greater need? Or, do I choose to live every day in love? Free, with nothing to fear, grateful for all God has given me and always having something to help my neighbor? Our me-first society has taught me how to be poor. It has taught me how to live in guilt and fear, with nothing to share. How do I learn to live in love?

Looking Beyond Ourselves

I think it helps to spend time reflecting upon the way things are. Life is so fast paced, we can fly along and hardly notice a thing. It's good to make the effort to notice how blessed I am, how many years God has given me, how precious every day is, the relationships I have, the abundance of food and clothing and shelter I enjoy, the physical and mental capabilities that are mine to command. Most of all, I can rejoice every day in the forgiveness, grace and hope that are mine in Christ. I can revel in the fact that I will never die, and I will inherit *everything*. It's good for us to count our blessings.

Then, we may be ready to notice the needs around us. Consider, first of all, needs you can do something about personally. Why send money overseas, if you have a hurting neighbor across the street or a hurting associate at work? In Jesus, God was very "hands on" with His mercy. He didn't heal people at a distance unless that was the only way. He preferred to touch them. Your love is a manifestation of God's love in Christ, so let people feel your love (and therefore, His) as personally as possible.

I'm not suggesting that we go out of our way to draw attention to ourselves. Jesus told us, "when you give to the needy, do not let your left hand know what your right hand is doing." (Matthew 6:3) Certainly, we should avoid trumpeting our generosity when making charitable donations. Jesus didn't mean, however, that there is anything wrong with helping a neighbor one-on-one. Maybe it's just spending a few moments talking, giving comfort, exploring or looking for ways you can help. Maybe it's taking over some food, sending a card, or watching their kids. Maybe it's giving them something encouraging to read, or taking some of their workload, or cutting their grass or giving them a ride to the doctor or to the airport. These are things that we owe our neighbors; responding to God's love for us by loving our fellowman is an ongoing debt. Paying that debt is a joy when we chose to live out of love instead of fear.

As you take time to ponder the way things are in the world, God may also bring to your mind general classes or types of people whom you can love. In particular, every trial you successfully endure through God's grace prepares you to minister to others in some way. I'm not suggesting that you go through hard times *just* for training. But God will use all of it *as* training because He wastes nothing.

Sometimes, the training is obvious: God brings you healing from the abandonment of divorce, and you can help others facing the same trial; God grants you deliverance from alcohol or drugs, and you can help others find the same freedom. Sometimes, the training is not so obvious: God overcomes your longstanding shame from being sexually abused as a child, and as a result, you simply have a heart for all children, to love those who are hurting in any way.

Let God raise to your attention the needs He has prepared you to meet. And rejoice that, while you used to live in exactly that kind of spiritual poverty, slavery or fear, God has saved you and healed you. Now you can do something to help. Yes, it's a debt that you owe, but it's a debt that feels so *right* to pay.

Thinking more broadly still, there's no way to think about the world as it really is, without contemplating the masses of people who are hurting in unthinkable ways. It's frightening to think how desperate needs create desperate people. And it's frustrating to realize that I cannot change the world and its brokenness. But God hasn't asked you to heal all the world's brokenness. Your only obligation to Him is to love, care, and do what you can for anyone you can. Love for my fellowman is a habit that gets stronger the more I use it. The important thing is to practice.

Money is a good place to start, because it's the easiest place to start. When you see a need that you can't meet personally because it's too big or too far away, put some money aside to help. One dollar will do something. Even if you're pretty strapped, you might be able to afford one dollar. Just put it aside in a special place. When you've accumulated, say $20, then use it to do something about the need you see. Just make a one time gift—make it anonymously, if you don't want to get on a mailing list. But make that gift an act of love; send it with a prayer for God to use it. I guarantee that no matter what else God is doing as He holds the world together, He will take note of your gift and He will use it. The first thing you'll notice is that your sense of guilt will start to evaporate. You guilt will fade, not because you feel proud of your tiny contribution, but because you will be too focused on helping to feel guilty. You'll be keeping informed about a need that has grabbed your soul. You will be researching good places to entrust your funds to help. You may even find yourself getting impatient, waiting for the next twenty dollars to accumulate, so you find a way to put ten dollars a month into your budget for that need. In only two months, you've got another twenty dollars to use. Before you know it, you're increasing that line item in your budget. Some-day, you might even find a way to budget some of your time and energy for those same people.

The key is simply to make your giving a conscious act of love. Give as one who is fulfilling an obligation, an obligation based on being loved by God. Enjoy that thought with each check. Let each gift be a conscious act of passing His love along. With every need you come across, look for an opportunity to exercise your stewardship and pay some of your debt. Do that with *every* need, every crisis you hear about among the people you work with, every tragic story you hear on the evening news, every scene of hopelessness and desperation around the world that comes into your living room. Some Christian may be praying for someone like you to take action. They're all tapped out and cannot help and they are praying for someone who can. If you are looking for ways to exercise your freedom to love, you will occasionally be the answer to someone else's prayer.

And what of all those times when you can't help? When, in transparent honesty before God, there truly is nothing you can do because *you* are all tapped out. What do you do then? You *don't* turn away. What you do is pray. Lift up dozens of sentence prayers every day. "God, I do not turn away from this needy person. I want to help; I want to help right now. All my resources are committed in ways that please you and I have nothing left. So I lift up this person to you, and ask you to raise up some Christian to help." By God's grace, there will be another Christian who is praying, "Lord, how would you have me pay my debt of love today?" and God will answer both of your prayers at the same time. The key is learning to live in love, not guilt or fear, but love. Stewardship is finding *joy* in managing what God has entrusted to me for His glory, and God has partially entrusted to me all my fellow human beings.

Lee Greenwood sang a love song called *IOU* that I have enjoyed singing to my wife, Micki.

> *IOU the sunlight in the morning*
> *And nights of honest loving that time can't take away*
> *And IOU more than life now more than ever*
> *I know that it's the sweetest debt I'll ever have to pay.*

I realize that Romans is not talking about romantic love. It is about love for strangers, for people I don't even like, indeed, for everyone. But I'm convinced that love for our fellowman is a debt that can become sweet to us, one that we can enjoy paying, day after day after day. I *do* owe my fellowman more than my life in this world, not because they are all my lovers but because Jesus is the Lover of my soul. He gave His life for me, so that I will live forever in a glorious blessedness I do not deserve. Love is a debt I can enjoy paying back, for it is how I express my gratitude to God. Caring for the well being of others is also how I experience my own well being. It's a way of celebrating my spiritual health and freedom and sense of richness. Love to my fellowman is part of my Christian stewardship.

One day, you will stand before God to joyfully give account of the stewardship of your life. Saved by grace alone. Loved as much as you can be loved, by grace alone. And every thing you have ever done for people who were not family, people you did not particularly like, people you may not even have personally known—every act of merciful good will you joyfully performed to pay a debt you felt inside—every one of those acts will proclaim to your Lord the genuine gratitude and appreciation you feel toward His Son and what He did for you. On that day, He will call forth the most loving among us and say, "You are truly faithful stewards. You used what I gave you to love as I loved you. Listen, I have a plan for a new world in which love is the way everything works. I want you to take the lead in building it with me!"

Prayer

Father, this aspect of our stewardship takes some getting used to. The idea of owing people love and good will and active mercy—owing it indiscriminately to everyone, whether they deserve it or not—this idea takes our breath away. Please help us to understand our moral debt to you, the love you have given us in Christ, and how He paid our debt on the cross. Overwhelm us with that love. Convince us of it. Conquer our shame, regret and guilt with your good will that just doesn't quit. Turn our guilt and fear into joy.

Father, we so easily listen to the worldly voices that divide and hoard and set us against each other. But we are yours, Father. We are Christians. There is no social barrier that can cut us off from our obligation to love our fellowman. We desire to pay our ongoing debt—not for merit, but for joy, compelled by the love of Christ. Help us to love like Him, we ask in His name. Amen.

Questions for Discussion

Romans 13:8-10

How is loving our fellowman a debt?

A debt to whom?
How is this debt related to God's Law?

How does Paul express the Golden Rule?
Apply it to...

the person who bags your groceries
your spouse, if married
people with whom you work
your next door neighbor
people in desperate crises on the local news
people in desperate need around the world

What would love require us to do for people who are chronically in need?

What does it take to love people who won't be paying us back?

If *millions* of Christians started living this way, how do you think it would effect the place of the church in our society?

May the Lord Rejoice in His Works

o o o o o o o o o o o o o o o o o o o o o o o o o o o o o o o o o
Praise the LORD, O my soul.

O LORD my God, you are very great;
    you are clothed with splendor and majesty.
He wraps himself in light as with a garment;
    he stretches out the heavens like a tent
    and lays the beams of his upper chambers on their waters.
He makes the clouds his chariot
    and rides on the wings of the wind.
He makes winds his messengers,
    flames of fire his servants.

He set the earth on its foundations;
    it can never be moved.
You covered it with the deep as with a garment;
    the waters stood above the mountains.
But at your rebuke the waters fled,
    at the sound of your thunder they took to flight;
they flowed over the mountains,
    they went down into the valleys,
    to the place you assigned for them.
You set a boundary they cannot cross;
    never again will they cover the earth.

He makes springs pour water into the ravines;
    it flows between the mountains.
They give water to all the beasts of the field;

the wild donkeys quench their thirst.
The birds of the air nest by the waters;
　　they sing among the branches.
He waters the mountains from his upper chambers;
　　the earth is satisfied by the fruit of his work.
He makes grass grow for the cattle,
　　and plants for man to cultivate—
　　bringing forth food from the earth:
wine that gladdens the heart of man,
　　oil to make his face shine,
　　and bread that sustains his heart.
The trees of the LORD are well watered,
　　the cedars of Lebanon that he planted.
There the birds make their nests;
　　the stork has its home in the pine trees.
The high mountains belong to the wild goats;
　　the crags are a refuge for the coneys.
The moon marks off the seasons,
　　and the sun knows when to go down.
You bring darkness, it becomes night,
　　and all the beasts of the forest prowl.
The lions roar for their prey
　　and seek their food from God.
The sun rises, and they steal away;
　　they return and lie down in their dens.
Then man goes out to his work,
　　to his labor until evening.

How many are your works, O LORD!
　　In wisdom you made them all;
　　the earth is full of your creatures.
There is the sea, vast and spacious,
　　teeming with creatures beyond number—
　　living things both large and small.

There the ships go to and fro,
    and the leviathan, which you formed to frolic there.

These all look to you
    to give them their food at the proper time.
When you give it to them,
    they gather it up;
when you open your hand,
    they are satisfied with good things.

When you hide your face,
    they are terrified;
when you take away their breath,
    they die and return to the dust.
When you send your Spirit,
    they are created,
    and you renew the face of the earth.

May the glory of the LORD endure forever;
    may the LORD rejoice in his works—
he who looks at the earth, and it trembles,
    who touches the mountains, and they smoke.

I will sing to the LORD all my life;
    I will sing praise to my God as long as I live.
May my meditation be pleasing to him,
    as I rejoice in the LORD.
But may sinners vanish from the earth
    and the wicked be no more.

Praise the LORD, O my soul.

Praise the LORD.

—Psalm 104

Stewardship is finding joy in managing what God has given for His glory. It involves managing that special temple which is our body, along with our renewed mind. It embraces our children specifically and all mankind generally. Psalm 104 broadens our scope even further, all the way to the creation itself, or at least that part of creation we have access to, this planet. What people today call "nature"—what the Bible calls "creation"—is perhaps the broadest context of our stewardship.

Psalm 104 portrays God as a caretaker, a servant who works hard and gets His hands dirty caring for the various life forms on this planet. It's clear that the one spoken of is, indeed, the Lord of glory. "O LORD my God, you are very great; you are clothed with splendor and majesty. He wraps himself in light as with a garment." "May the glory of the LORD endure forever; may the LORD rejoice in his works—he who looks at the earth, and it trembles, who touches the mountains, and they smoke." This is the Lord God Almighty we are talking about.

But the Lord God revealed in the Bible is no ivory tower, Zen-like figure of distant contemplation. The Lord is pictured as the Creator, in the sense of a builder, the builder of this planet. "He stretches out the heavens like a tent and lays the beams of his upper chambers on their waters." "He set the earth on its foundations; it can never be moved. You covered it with the deep as with a garment; the waters stood above the mountains. But at your rebuke the waters fled…they went down into the valleys, to the place you assigned for them." You can almost see the Lord framing the sky, laying foundations, digging and carving the landscape. And once made, the Lord turns from Creator to Sustainer, from Builder to Caretaker. "He makes springs pour water into the ravines; it flows between the mountains. They give water to all the beasts of the field; the wild donkeys quench their thirst…He waters the mountains from his upper chambers; the earth is satisfied by the fruit of his work. He makes grass grow for the cattle…The trees of the LORD are well watered."

The God with Dirt Under His Fingernails

Is this the way you see your Lord, as one who daily waters His earth? Do you ever water your garden? God pictures Himself as doing exactly the same thing. Clearly, God loves this garden we call Planet Earth. Clearly, God loves all the creatures He has made—including mankind, but not only mankind. "The trees of the LORD are well watered…There the birds make their nests; the stork has its home in the pine trees. The high mountains belong to the wild goats…The lions roar for their prey and seek their food from God…There is the sea, vast and spacious, teeming with creatures beyond number—living things both large and small…and the leviathan, which you formed to frolic there. These all look to you to give them their food at the proper time…How many are your works, O LORD! In wisdom you made them all; the earth is full of your creatures."

In the book of Job, you sense the same loving pride and joy God has for the world and the creatures He has made. There, God speaks lovingly of how lightning is generated and the jet stream scatters the wind, how rain carves the earth's surface and the ground is blessed with dew and frost. The Bible doesn't approach the Earth as an impersonal, meaningless accident of nature. It is the personal pride of the Living God who delights to daily take part in its wonders. In Job 38-40, we read, "Who provides food for the raven when its young cry out to God?…Who let the wild donkey go free?…I gave him the wasteland as his home, the salt flats as his habitat."

God is much more involved with His creatures than we are, "Do you know when the mountain goats give birth? Do you watch when the doe bears her fawn? Do you count the months till they bear?…Does the hawk take flight by your wisdom and spread his wings toward the south? Does the eagle soar at your command and build his nest on high?" God delights in just watching His creatures be themselves, "[the wild donkey] laughs at the commotion in the town; he does not hear a driver's shout. He ranges the hills for his pasture and searches for any green thing…The wings of the ostrich flap joyfully…She lays her eggs on the ground and lets them warm in the sand, unmindful that a foot may crush them, that some wild animal may trample them…she cares not that her labor was in vain, for God did not endow her with wisdom or give her a share of good sense. Yet when she spreads her feathers to run, she laughs at horse and rider…[The horse] paws fiercely, rejoicing in his strength…he laughs at fear, afraid of nothing…In frenzied excitement he eats up the ground…Look at the behemoth…What strength he has in his loins…yet his Maker can approach him…He ranks first among the works of God."

What does that do to human ego? There are days when God can enjoy His hippopotamus and say that *he* ranks first among His works!

Why We Are Here

Why did God make mankind? To glorify Himself, yes, but how? The Bible first addresses the reason for our existence in a very practical way, "Now the LORD God had planted a garden in the east, in Eden…And the LORD God made all kinds of trees grow out of the ground—trees that were pleasing to the eye and good for food…The LORD God took the man and put him in the Garden of Eden to work it and take care of it." (Genesis 2:8-15) Humanity was made to take care of God's garden. I know that we like to think that the garden—or actually the whole planet—was made for us. But in Genesis, it's the other way around: we were made to take care of God's garden.

The Garden of Eden was what we would call today a prototype. On a wild planet teaming with life, God created a space of order. God improved the wilderness according to two criteria: whatever was "good for food" and "pleasing to the eye." Eden was more productive and more beautiful than was nature in the raw. It was neither a city (as we know it) nor a zoo, but rather a habitat more beneficial to all its life forms than any untouched wilderness could be. A place particularly fruitful for mankind, so we could multiply, fill the earth, and turn the entire planet into an Eden-like environment, much more beautiful and fruitful than the chaotic wilderness.

This creative, caretaking dominion is the context in which "the image of God" is defined. Being in God's image defines our ability and responsibility to imitate God as a creator and caretaker. God made a vast wilderness of stars and nebula and dust. In the middle of this wilderness, He formed a planet teeming with life, the most beautiful and fruitful place in the universe. We are supposed to glorify God by doing the same thing in miniature. Our planet was created a wilderness, and we were charged to make the whole place more beautiful and more fruitful for every creature.

Eden was a prototype for us to study and expand creatively. This Earth was not made for us; it was made for God. God made us to care for it and develop it. Do you find the role of caretaker demeaning? God doesn't. Psalm 104 portrays Him going out every morning to water His planet. In God's economy, the last are first, and the servant is King. God watches over the entire Earth. If we are trusted to imitate Him, it is the highest calling of any creature. Our identity and purpose are bound up with this place. God *loves* this planet and its creatures. It's not just scenery, some backdrop or stage upon which we dance to our own music. God made us to care for this place because He loves it. He made us to be caretakers.

You see this original purpose reflected in Old Testament Law. For example, the purpose of the Sabbath is to affirm that God still owns the creation. Each week, all the earth is to rest as God did on the Sabbath, finding its joyful purpose in Him. "The seventh day is a Sabbath to the LORD your God. On it you shall not do any work, neither you, nor your son or daughter…nor your animals." (Exodus 20:10) Note how the Sabbath included domesticated animals. "A righteous man cares for the needs of his animal." (Proverbs 12:10) One of the reasons Israel was cast into exile was that it would not allow *the land* to rest; they would not give the land its Sabbaths. They treated the land as if it belonged to them, to use as they saw fit. God said that it belongs to Him, and He would hold them accountable to use it as He saw fit (cf. Leviticus 26:33-35).

God's original intent was to work with Adam, Eve and their children as a Father, teaching us all about this wonderful world and how to care for it. He would put His hands around ours as we tie up vines, gentle horses and design ecosystems. He would instruct us as we study how weather works, and stars are born, and atoms interact. All this, with a view of expanding our initial Eden using the same two criteria of that prototype: make everything fruitful, and make everything beautiful.

In this way, we were to lead the whole Earth in its praise to God. "Praise the LORD from the earth, you great sea creatures and all ocean depths, lightning and hail, snow and clouds, stormy winds that do his bidding, you mountains and all hills, fruit trees and all cedars, wild animals and all cattle, small creatures and fly-ing birds…Let them praise the name of the LORD, for his name alone is exalted; his splendor is above the earth and the heavens." (Psalm 148:7-13)

Sin came into this world when we rejected our purpose to care for and expand His Garden. On that day, we stopped being stewards of this planet, and became mere users. Sin is a self-centered human orgy that sees this earth as something to consume, not something to love and develop for God's sake.

The Lord God built Himself a magnificent home in the midst of this wild and wonderful universe, a home where chaos is turned into domestic bliss. He created children just for the joy of sharing this bliss. And what have we done? We have trashed His house, and we go on trashing it. We trash what God loves, and then we wonder why He is angry, why He will judge us and one day wipe our impact off of this planet. How would you feel if someone you trusted trashed your house?

It's hard for us to fully appreciate what our sin and its consequences have done to the Lord's masterpiece. "The creation was subjected to frustration...bondage to decay...groaning as in the pains of childbirth right up to the present time." (Romans 8:20-22) The Bible says that after our Fall into sin, God put the fear of mankind into the animals; even cultivated plants resist us with thorns. We ourselves know pain and death. Even if you have enjoyed the Grand Canyon or the Outer Banks, you have never seen this planet the way it was supposed to be. We've ruined it.

Biblical redemption is not just about the salvation of mankind. It's about the restoration of the entire created order. "The creation waits in eager expectation for the sons of God to be revealed." (Romans 8:19) The creation is waiting for its caretakers—*us*—to come to our senses by the grace of God. There will be a new heaven and a new earth, and the new earth will be the home of righteousness. Jesus Christ came to redeem a fallen humanity, calling out a multitude from sin and judgment and death to joyful obedience, eternal acceptance and everlasting life. But before He is finished, He will make *all* things new. "God was pleased...through him to reconcile to himself all things, whether things on earth or things in heaven, by making peace through his blood, shed on the cross." (Colossians 1:19-20)

It's not just humanity that rejoices in Christ. "Let the heavens rejoice, let the earth be glad; let the sea resound, and all that is in it; let the fields be jubilant, and everything in them. Then all the trees of the forest will sing." (Psalm 96:11-12) "Let the rivers clap their hands, let the mountains sing together for joy; let them sing before the LORD, for he comes to judge the earth. He will judge the world in righteousness." (Psalm 98:8-9) Or, as Isaac Watts summarized in one of our favorite Christmas carols, "Joy to the world! The Savior reigns; Let men their songs employ; while fields and floods, rocks, hills and plains Repeat the sounding joy...No more let sins and sorrows grow, nor thorns infest the ground; He comes to make His blessing flow far as the curse is found."

Christ's redemption begins with the salvation of sinners who repent and trust Him, but it will not end until He returns and His blessing flows as far as the curse is found. It will touch the fields and hills and plains, the ravens and wild donkeys and tall cedars that God so loves. Stewardship is joyfully managing this planet God has given us for His glory.

Learning to Tend the Garden

What aspect of our stewardship could be more difficult, especially for us in our culture? In some ways, America is a leader in conservation and national parks. We have developed wonderful technologies to make our nation more fruitful and beautiful. But we are a society which—more than any other society in history—is built on the idea of consumption. Our economy thrives on people consuming as much as possible. The American citizen is referred to as "the consumer" (Just *think* about how God feels about that). To oppose such an identity seems un-American. This is understandable, since we have based our jobs, livelihoods, transportation…our entire economy on personal consumption.

How are we supposed to learn the joy of managing this planet to God's glory in such an environment? Especially when so many of us conservative Christians seem oblivious to our God-given identity as caretakers of this planet and the life it shelters? Christian conservatives emphasize that mankind has dominion over the earth. Since God made mankind in His image, we are therefore more important than, say, the Florida grasshopper sparrow when it comes to building condos on the beach.

Yes, mankind *is* the most important life form on the planet; Jesus said one of us is worth many sparrows in the sight of God. But Jesus also said, "Yet not one [sparrow] is forgotten by God" (Luke 12:6), and He expects us to feel the same way. Dominion is not cruel dictatorship. God did not design mankind to bully and abuse the other creatures. We are allowed to eat animals, and the growth of humanity implies the need to reorder habitats. But God never intended for us to run roughshod over the plants and animals He took pains to create.

God goes out every day to water and care for His planet; that's how Psalm 104 pictures Him. He is looking for children who enjoy doing the same thing. So, how can we learn to love our stewardship of the planet?

The obvious place to start is in our homes. Global warming or cooling or whatever is too abstract and too distant as a place to begin. We need to start in that little extension of Eden we call "home." That is what a house or estate is; it is our little extension of Eden. It is where we each have an opportunity to transform the wilderness so as to make our little corner of the Earth both fruitful and beautiful.

Home is where we should be most fruitful. It is the place to bear and raise children, teaching them to love this planet as God loves it.

Home is a place to teach the love of all kinds of tools, from power saws to word processors to paint brushes, depending on our gifts. My Dad taught me to be comfortable around hand tools as I was growing up. (I still can't use them all that well, but at least I'm comfortable with them!) I'm more at home using a computer creatively. Right now, I'm finishing up a hymn I've been working on for over a year. I can't play an instrument, but I can play a computer. Micki is good with both computers and crafts. The last time my married daughter was home for a visit, she and Micki experimented with a new cooking style—cooking is another tool-craft.

Of course, we can control our use of energy in our homes. We can have a great lifestyle and still be mindful of our environment. There are so many things we can do. I've been mowing our small lawn with an electric mower for years. You know why? According to CNN, a single two-cycle lawn mower engine puts out more pollution than 73 new automobiles!

Home is where we learn to care about the local environment. I grew up here on the Chesapeake Bay. I remember crabbing through the seaweed. Most of the seaweed and the ecosystem it represents is gone now, along with many of the crabs. So much lost in just one generation. Just rethinking how we fertilize our lawns can have a major impact on the future of the Bay. Home is a place where we can be stewards of the earth's fruitfulness.

And, of course, home is a also place where we create beauty and harmony. A home's décor does not have to be expensive, but it should be thoughtful. It should resemble a garden, not a wilderness. I'm not speaking of plants particularly, but of order, composition and tasteful adornment. Home is where children can learn to care for animals, if only for a pet or two. Our pets and azaleas are not more important than we are, but we are responsible to take care of them. It's such a tiny step. Ultimately, God will hold us accountable for all of His creatures, every Sequoia, every salmon, every rose…and yes, every sparrow (He hasn't forgotten a single one). God asks us to care for this world responsibly, respectfully, lovingly, as if it all belonged to Him. Because it does, and He loves it.

Beyond our homes, we need to think of our careers in terms of our stewardship of this planet. When you think of what college to attend and what major to choose, try to include your stewardship of the planet in your career goals. It's not always easy to relate that responsibility to your career, but you must try. And within every career, or every job, there are always ways you can find to be a better steward of this wonderful world. Recycling obviously comes to mind, as does carpooling, or choosing office supplies wisely. Perhaps your organization would like to investigate renewable energy resources or sponsor an animal shelter. You could honor your Lord by taking the lead in such initiatives.

One final application: I think we need to bring our sense of stewardship of the planet with us into our politics. Be warned, however, that responsibly developing this planet will often take us outside of party platforms. One side may argue that we must conserve nature just the way it is. That's not always true. God expects us to improve the wilderness and make it like Eden. He expects us to make the wilderness productive and even more beautiful, so we can use the Earth for our benefit. We *are* worth many sparrows, and stewards have the right to benefit from what they manage.

But the other side may argue that the immediate needs of humanity (jobs, homes, energy) outweigh the long range needs of forests and caribou and air quality. That's not always true, either. God holds us responsible for the air and caribou and forests. They do not exist only for our use; *they belong to Him*, down to the last sparrow, and we are entrusted with their care.

Maybe the best answer is not so simplistic either way. Maybe political responsibility for our environment requires that people with different viewpoints work together and see the value of each other's arguments. Maybe it requires Christians to speak up with a heavenly perspective that brings a more reasoned and responsible view to earthly matters.

And as always when it comes to stewardship, the key ingredient for us is joy. Loving this gorgeous planet and all the life on it reflects the character of Almighty God as much as anything I know. It's part of what makes us in His image. Caring for, appreciating, enjoying this Earth is an essential aspect of our humanity. The further we get from it—the further we let our children get from it—the less we'll remember who we are.

In her last TV role, "Stone Pillow" of 1985, Lucile Ball portrayed a homeless but fiercely independent bag lady dealing with an idealistic volunteer from a homeless shelter. We learn how she lost her husband, children and house, ending up on the street. We also see how she lost most of her humanity along the way, living without purpose in a paved universe. The last scene was unforgettable for me. Through the efforts of that volunteer, the bag lady found a home again, a house outside the city. The final scene finds her in a back yard, with tears of joy running down her face as she thrusts her hands in the real dirt of a real garden.

Having dominion is not a license to bully and abuse. It means imitating our God, who goes out everyday to water the beasts of the field, tend the grass, count the months until the deer give birth…and wait for His children to join Him.

One day, we'll stand before the Lord, laying at His feet all the fruit of our stewardship. Saved by grace alone, and loved perfectly and eternally for Christ's sake, we will illustrate from our lives how much we *enjoy* serving Him. On that day, He will ask some of us to come forward. "I've watched you. You treated the Earth as if it belonged to me. Now, I want to complete the project I began long ago. And I want to entrust the biggest projects to sons and daughters who share my happiness in making this a very special place. Let's get started!"

Prayer

Father, in case we haven't said so to you before, we feel it is a great privilege to be made in your image. You are quite a marvelous Creator and Caretaker of this beautiful jewel of a planet. We don't know what it is like in Heaven, where you rule over angelic beings. We're sure that's nice, too. But you have given us human beings one fantastic home. We make songs about purple mountains and fruited plains, but it's hard to find words to do justice to this place.

You've also given us a lot of wonderful companions here—animals and plants of every kind and description. Even now, we haven't discovered them all. To think that you have entrusted each one to our care is amazing.

Father, we know you don't want us living naked in caves, eating roots and berries. You love the way we have invented machines and electronics. But we confess that sin has rotted out our identity as stewards of this planet. We've almost forgotten what you put us here for.

To think that our destiny in Christ is to rediscover all this! To think that one day animals will not fear us, or we them. To think that one day, we will understand nature almost as well as you do. This is exciting, and we want to get started now. We don't want to wait until this phase of history is over. We want to taste your kingdom now—in our homes and in our careers and even on a broader scale, if we can. We want the world to see how fruitful and beautiful faith in Christ can make this world. Help us to do this, Father, in every nation, until your Son returns and all creation praises you. We ask for His sake. Amen.

Questions for Discussion

Psalm 104

Consider how Psalm 104 portrays God as…

a builder
a caretaker

Give examples from the psalm that indicate how the Lord feels about…

animals
plants

What place does the psalm give mankind in the scheme of things?

Describe our approach to life on this planet, if we had the same attitude toward it that God has.

How would such an attitude inform or impact…

our career?
our property?
our politics?

The Church of the Living God

o o o o o o o o o o o o o o o o o o o o o o o o o o o o o o o o

Although I hope to come to you soon, I am writing you these
instructions so that, if I am delayed, you will know how people
ought to conduct themselves in God's household, which is the
church of the living God, the pillar and foundation of the truth.

—1 Timothy 3:14-15

Stewardship is joyfully managing what God has given us for His glory. So far,
we've considered our stewardship of resources that have eternal value: our bodies
and minds, our children, our neighbors, and the planet itself. Today, we look at
the last item in this section of our study, the stewardship of Christ's church. The
Church is another thing that is of eternal value, and our stewardship of it will follow us into the age to come.

The English word "church" translates a Greek word for "assembly." It was used
in New Testament times to describe a public assembly of citizens. More importantly, it was the word used to translate the Old Testament word for "congregation," that referred to all the people of Israel. The word describes a group that is
called out together for some purpose. God's church is that group of people called
out from the world to belong to Him, as the Apostle Peter said, "a chosen people…a people belonging to God, that you may declare the praises of him who
called you out of darkness into his wonderful light." (1 Peter 2:9)

Sometimes, when we think of church, we think of it in its most abstract and least
visible form. We think of the Body of Christ, the universal Church, the entire
group of believers from every age and around the world. This is a group mostly
invisible to our eyes; it's so spread out, and many are already in heaven. Obviously, Paul is not thinking of the universal church in this text. In 1 Timothy, he
is describing the work and the selection of individual elders and deacons. He's
addressing very concrete and hands-on matters of church life. This is the church

most visible, local congregations linked together in mutual accountability. If we are part of the church, and God calls the church to be something special, then making the church that "something" is part of our stewardship.

God's Vision for the Church

In our text, Paul gives two images or metaphors that describe what the real-world church is to be like. First, Paul says that the church is supposed to be a household, God's household, to be exact. God created all mankind, but humanity rebelled against God and broke away from Him. In His infinite mercy, God set about the task of calling back a large multitude of such rebellious sinners to Himself. Through the grace of Christ's cross and resurrection, and through faith in His work, individual men, women and children are reconciled to God. Each one becomes part of a spiritual family linked together by Jesus Christ and His Spirit. "To all who received [Christ], to those who believed in his name, he gave the right to become children of God." (John 1:12) "For...you received the Spirit of sonship. And by him we cry, 'Abba, Father.' The Spirit himself testifies with our spirit that we are God's children." (Romans 8:15-16)

Redemption is God's work of creating for Himself a human family, a household of people reconciled to Him. You can actually see the concept physically modeled in the Old Testament. When God called Israel out of Egypt to be His congregation or church, He had them set up a tent, called a Tabernacle, in the center of the camp. He caused His name to "dwell" in the tent by manifesting His presence with a supernatural light. The lights were always on in God's house. The Lord wanted all His children to live with Him in His house, but the tent simply wasn't big enough. So, He asked for the firstborn of each home to come and serve Him at His tent, live with Him in His house and represent each family. But even that arrangement would be too burdensome and unwieldy, so one tribe, Levi, was set apart to take the place of the firstborn of every home. Some of them became priests. The point is that in ancient Israel, God set up a house and *all* the people lived with Him, represented by the tribe of Levi. Therefore, with the Tabernacle and Temple that followed, God was not just portraying His *house*; He was portraying His *household.*

That's what the concrete, visible church is to be: God's household in this world. God exists everywhere, but He causes His name to live with us. His Spirit lives with us; He lives in our relationships, as His family, His household. Every one of us in the church is privileged to treat God as our Heavenly Father, and since we have the same Father, we are automatically of the same family. The Apostle John states, "Whoever loves God must also love his brother…everyone who loves the father loves his child as well." (1 John 4:21-5:1)

The Bible says that Christians the world over and throughout time are spiritually related to each other. In the real-world church, we actually learn to live that way. "Be devoted to one another in brotherly love." (Romans 12:10) We are told to "exhort [an older man] as if he were your father. Treat younger men as brothers, older women as mothers, and younger women as sisters, with absolute purity." (1 Timothy 5) The church should be a place in which God's presence is so palpable that His presence is in every relationship. In the church, Christians learn to think, feel and act as God's family.

The second way Paul describes the church is quite different. This time the image is not of a group of people, but rather a building which houses the truth. He speaks of "the church of the living God, the pillar and foundation of the truth." Here, the image is not one of relationships, but of some kind of structure. A structure supplying both a foundation and pillars for the truth. The church forms a firm base, an unshakable foundation upon which the truth can rest, pillars upon which truth can rise and take shape.

God revealed to us the truth of who He is through Israel, and ultimately through the Christ. God had this truth enscripturated, or written down. The church provides a structure in which that sacred Scripture is preserved, a structure in which God's truth fully assumes its proper shape. This revelation includes the character of God, the world and humanity, as well as the nature of sin and redemption. When these truths are supported, they build upon one another to give us an entire superstructure of thought, a view of life and reality that fits together. They give us a world view that integrates our understanding, values, behavior—*everything*. There is nothing else like it. There is nothing that can rival the biblical world view when it comes to making sense out of life and giving all of life meaning. To preserve and teach this truth, the church creates concrete expressions of doctrine and exercises discipline to maintain that teaching among local assemblies.

We Christians are stewards of an institution we call the church, a home for the Body of Christ. It is an institution in which people adopt the roles of family members and work to faithfully define and proclaim God's revelation. Like any institution, the church is bigger than the people in it at any given time. The church is a structure of relationships and purpose passed on from one generation of believers to another, until God's people are complete and Christ returns. At any point in history, it is God's household on earth, and the chosen structure for preserving His truth.

Our Vision of the Church

Let's look at each side of that stewardship. First, Christians in the institutional church are responsible to assume certain roles, so that the Body of Christ can assume a tangible form in the world. When you think of roles in the church, you may think of the offices of pastor, elder and deacon. Paul speaks of these offices in this very chapter, but these are not the roles that define the essential character of the church. In Christ's church, everyone is to assume the role of a family member. The Lord calls us to become His children through Christ. In the church, we learn to actually behave and think of ourselves that way.

My primary role in my congregation is to be a member of the church family. For some, I am a son, for you are old enough to be my father or mother. I am to honor you as a mother or a father. You deserve that kind of tender courtesy. I can come to you for advice, and I can watch out for your welfare as you get along in years. For others, I am a father, for you are young enough to be my children. You must treat me with respect because in the church I am like a parent to you. I must watch over you and train you and encourage you, lead you to Christ and prepare you for life. For most, I am a brother, for we are roughly within the same generation. As brothers and sisters, we bring each other meals when we are sick. We share our personal achievements and personal trials. And of course, we get together at our Parent's house, especially on Sunday, just to enjoy being His family.

Secondly, the church not only lives as a spiritual family, but it also acts as an institution to carry God's truth through the centuries. The purpose of the visible, hands-on church is to perpetuate God's truth in this world. We must preserve, protect and defend it, spread it around the world and pass it on to the next spiritual generation. Note that Paul does not say that the truth is the foundation of the church, but that the church is the foundation and pillar of the truth. The truth comes from God, of course, but the church is charged to faithfully preserve and teach it in this world throughout history until Christ returns. As this letter draws to a close, Paul will say, "Timothy, guard what has been entrusted to your care." (1 Timothy 6:20) In that verse, he goes on to warn Timothy to be constantly vigilant against attempts to change or warp or discard or reshape that truth.

Unfortunately, this is mostly an internal struggle, in that the greatest threats to the truth do not come from the world. The world burns Bibles and imprisons Christians, but they can't change our message that way. It's when people inside the church, church leaders, subject the Word of God to the fashions of the day—that is the real danger. The real threat is when seminaries, church boards and pastors lay aside the Bible to please man or please their colleagues or please themselves. And who is responsible to stop this, to preserve and display the truth accurately? *You* are responsible, Christian. It is part of your stewardship, and mine.

This stewardship of the Church as an institution has never been more important than it is today. We live in a culture that is forgetting what it means to be human. Biblical truth preserved for ages is being cast aside. Fading away is the bedrock understanding of humanity as created in God's image to express His character in the universe. Along with it is vanishing an understanding of sin that makes sense out of our guilt. Above all, we are losing hope—not only in everlasting life, but hope that life has meaning at all. In his book, *Rumors of Another World*, Philip Yancey writes, "Most people in history have experienced this world with its pleasures and pains, its births and deaths and loves and passages, as linked to a sacred, invisible world. No longer, or not for many, at least. Now we are born, play, work, accumulate possessions, relate to one another, and die with no consolation that what we do matters ultimately or has any meaning beyond what we assign it."

This world desperately needs a faithful church. One that upholds the revelation of God with humble faith, intellectual integrity and warm compassion. A church in which people become a functioning family under their Heavenly Father. The world thinks the church is irrelevant, but it remains humanity's only hope.

Making it Real

God wants the Body of Christ to take tangible form here on earth. He wants it made visible and concrete, with real people, relationships, clear theology and teaching. You embrace your stewardship of the church when you say: "I'm not satisfied with theoretical Christianity. I want something tangible. It is God's will for me to create something tangible, something that makes the truth He has revealed visible." Sure, all Christians are mystically related to each other, but are we going to actually *be* family? Sure, the Bible is God's revelation to mankind, but are we going to make sure that it is accurately taught and proclaimed? The church is part of our stewardship.

So, let's find joy in the church by adopting the roles that He designed for us, the *family* roles of parent, child or sibling. Let's start thinking of ourselves that way. Make the Body of Christ visible in your congregation. Think about the spiritual parents in your congregation, fathers and mothers in the faith. How many of their faces do you see on a Sunday morning? How many do you know? When you pass in the hallway or between services, treat them with respect. Greet them, speak to them a moment, treat them as a father or mother. Ask their advice about life (they've had a lot more experience). Pray for their increasing infirmities. Help them out with chores they find too difficult. As part of your stewardship of the church, you could be a great son or daughter.

Think about your spiritual children in your congregation, covenant children your are responsible to help raise. How many of them do you know? You are, in a way, godparents to them all. Think of all the achievements and milestones you can enjoy helping them achieve. Adopt other families in the church with children the same age as yours, so our kids can become friends and support each other's faith. Look for ways to encourage and invest in church programs dedicated to our children and young people. As part of your stewardship of the church, you could be a great parent.

Think of your spiritual sisters and brothers in this congregation. They sit around you every Sunday, along with welcome guests. We have a responsibility to share our personal lives, with all our successes and trials. We get to watch out for church folk who are alone on holidays, and invite them to join us. We get to stay up all night in the hospital, rejoice at graduations and wedding receptions, and mourn together at funerals. We get to pray together and encourage each other with wisdom. We get to take each other meals and loan each other transportation and work hard to help each other escape the sin that holds us back. As part of your stewardship of the church, you could be a great brother or sister.

And Christian, let's find joy in managing the church God has given us by guarding what has been entrusted to us, and keeping the church as the foundation and pillar of the truth. You've heard, "All that is necessary for evil to triumph is for good people to do nothing." That's not just true of nations; its true of churches, too. How do you think so many denominations have wandered away from biblical truth? Because not enough faithful Christians guarded what was entrusted to them.

I recently got back from a week at the General Assembly of our denomination. It is my responsibility as an elder to represent you and our Presbytery in overseeing the work of our denomination. This year I was on the committee that reviewed the work of our seminary. We examined the minutes of all board meetings, we interviewed the Seminary President and satisfied ourselves that this institution that trains many of our pastors is remaining faithful to the Word. In our Presbytery, your elders review the work our churches do together such as planting churches, and we examine men who wish to be ordained to gospel ministry. This year, I led the Shepherding Committee that works with pastors and churches in trouble. As Pastor, that's part of *my* stewardship of the church.

You guard the truth by becoming familiar with church doctrine, and holding this congregation accountable to biblical standards. You guard the truth by making sure the men you elect to leadership love God's Word, love Christ and love His church. Some of you can guard the truth by cultivating your love for Christ and His Word, and aspiring to leadership yourself. You guard the truth by keeping abreast of what is happening in your congregation, by coming to congregational meetings, asking questions and encouraging the staff. You guard the truth by keeping current not just with your local church, but your denomination, and you get involved if you see your denomination straying from the doctrine entrusted to it by God. Guarding the truth is part of your stewardship.

We live in a day when many believers in this country are mourning the lack of stewardship that allowed denominations with glorious histories to theologically disintegrate. It was a lack of stewardship that allowed foundations and pillars to crack, so that truth fell to the ground. Pray for godly minorities in those denominations as they gauge how much more of this battle they can take before they leave to join more faithful institutions. Support and strengthen your denomination to remain faithful as long as possible. Wouldn't it be great if your church could run the race all the way to the end, and be among those that faithfully greet our Lord at His return?

One day, you will stand before your Lord, enjoying His good pleasure and looking forward to an eternity of creative, blessed living. There will be great projects to accomplish, noble and wonderful things to achieve in our dominion of the new earth. God is looking now, right now, for good stewards He can trust to manage those projects, beloved children whose greatest joy is to manage what He gives them for His glory. He is looking for children who, more than anything else, enjoy working with Him. On that great day, He will call some of us to come forward, "I've been watching you. You share my passion to turn this bunch into a real family. And you have guarded my Word. You treasured it and passed it on to the generation that followed you, so my will could be known by all who cared to know it. Well, here is a whole new world, ready to become what I have dreamed it to be. I want you to join me in leading the way."

Prayer

Father, thank you for allowing us to be part of your church, this millennia-spanning institution designed to house a spiritual family drawn together by your truth. Please forgive us for any ways we have taken our stewardship lightly, so that through our lack of commitment we've allowed your church to languish and fall short of its potential.

Lord, regardless of whatever offices or positions in the church we may or may not have, help us to take up the roles that really matter to you—our place in this family as sons and daughters, brothers and sisters, and mothers and fathers. May we experience a taste of your eternal design among people who are related to each other because they belong to you.

And Lord, in a day when so many parts of your institutional church are stumbling and stammering for lack of biblical truth, help us to become even more faithful with your Word. May your truth penetrate our hearts, convict us of our sin, encourage us with your grace and inspire us with your perfect plan. Help us to be faithful to guard what you have entrusted to us.

Thank you for your church, dear Father. We are delighted to be stewards of it, for Jesus' sake. Amen.

Questions for Discussion

1 Timothy 3:14-15

What two images or metaphors concerning the church does Paul suggest?

Read 1 Timothy 5:1-2.

How is the church a kind of household?
Consider the sampling of family roles mentioned 1 Timothy 5:1-2, and suggest others.
What responsibilities would you associate with each of these roles in the church?

Read the first sentence of 1 Timothy 6:20.

Whose responsibility is it to guard the truth entrusted to the church?
How well do you think the contemporary church is doing at upholding and preserving the truths of the Scripture?
Paul's language suggests the structure of a building. Using that metaphor, what kind of structure does the church need in order to guard the truth?

A Time for Everything

o o o o o o o o o o o o o o o o o o o o o o o o o o o o o o o o o

There is a time for everything, and a season for every activity under heaven: a time to be born and a time to die, a time to plant and a time to uproot, a time to kill and a time to heal, a time to tear down and a time to build, a time to weep and a time to laugh, a time to mourn and a time to dance, a time to scatter stones and a time to gather them, a time to embrace and a time to refrain, a time to search and a time to give up, a time to keep and a time to throw away, a time to tear and a time to mend, a time to be silent and a time to speak, a time to love and a time to hate, a time for war and a time for peace.

—Ecclesiastes 3:1-8

Up to now in our study of stewardship, we have considered the things we can joyfully manage for God that have eternal significance: our bodies and minds, our children and our neighbors, this planet and the church. Everything will be transformed when Christ returns, but one way or another, all these things have eternal value. God is looking for stewards who take joy in managing them for His glory.

Now, we'll begin to look at some other things we manage, tools loaned to us in this life with which to manage all the things we have discussed. These tools are extremely important; we need them to accomplish our stewardship. But unlike the things we have already looked at, these tools will *not* follow us into eternity. They are like a disposable foam brush. I need such a brush to stain a small home project I plan to make as a gift. When I'm done, I will give this gift to someone I love and throw the brush away. I need it now to prepare my gift. But it is not the gift itself, and I will discard it when I'm done.

Up to now, we've studied what we will give to God when Christ returns. Now, we will look at three tools we use in this life to prepare those offerings: time, money, and spiritual gifts. Our first subject is the stewardship of time, and our text is a famous piece from Ecclesiastes.

Seasons of Life

"There is a time for everything." As the Preacher (I believe him to be Solomon) considers the futility of so many of our actions, he stresses that we would do better to coordinate our attitudes and our choices with the various occasions of life. Different situations brought into our lives by God's providence call for different responses.

The text begins, "a time to be born and a time to die." Many translators prefer, "a time to give birth and a time to die." That is, there is a time in life when one should focus on starting a family and there is a time to put one's affairs in order and prepare for death.

The next three pairs develop this idea of creating and destroying: "a time to plant and a time to uproot…a time to kill and a time to heal…a time to tear down and a time to build." We must understand that the verbs chosen here are used symbolically throughout the Old Testament. God plants the heavens and uproots the nations. God builds the throne of David and tears down Jehoshaphat's schemes. The adulteress kills the virtue of young men; healing can bless the soul as well as body. In other words, Solomon is not thinking of specific actions, but rather of those occasions in life when it is appropriate to begin new things, and other times when it is appropriate to end what has gone before.

As we go on, we see that Solomon not only deals with actions, but also with emotions: "a time to weep and a time to laugh…a time to mourn and a time to dance." The feelings we cultivate on the inside, and the way we express our emotions on the outside should correspond to what is happening in our lives. We live best when we appropriately respond to God's providences.

Finally, Solomon applies the same thinking to our relationships: "a time to scatter and a time to gather…a time to embrace and a time to refrain…a time to search and a time to give up…a time to keep and a time to throw away…a time to tear and a time to mend…a time to be silent and a time to speak…a time to love and a time to hate…a time for war and a time for peace." Family love, erotic love, relations between individuals and nations—sometimes we need to seek out relationships and bond together, at other times we need to distance ourselves or even enter into conflict.

Actions, emotions and relationships. We should purposefully choose how we live in accordance with the seasons of life that come upon us. "There is a time for everything." The sense of the Hebrew is that there is an *appointed* time for everything. Not only in the sense that God providentially oversees what happens *to* us, but also in the sense that we are responsible to choose an appropriate *response*. "There is…a season for every activity under heaven." Life is not all love and embracing and building up. There are times for those things, but there is a season for every activity. There are also times for war and mourning, or tearing down to prepare for something new. These "negative" actions and feelings, the breaking up of these relationships are not pleasant, but sometimes they are necessary. They are the right thing to do…at the time.

Biblical Time Management

Solomon had a very different approach to time management than we do. Keep in mind that Solomon must have been one of the busiest people in history. He oversaw the courts, conducted huge building projects, pursued complex diplomatic ties and conducted extensive lectures in the natural sciences. I'm sure he had his version of a PDA in the form of efficient servants. I dare say that Solomon accomplished more in his career than any of us probably will. But for Solomon, time management was much, much more than scheduling. For Solomon, *when* was tied to *why*, whether or not a given task was *appropriate* at the given time. Just because lots of things presented themselves as urgent, that did not mean that Solomon put them all on his schedule. Solomon was careful to sense the season. Was it a time for planting, or uprooting? A time for war, or a time for peace? Only then would Solomon the Wise start to fill in his schedule.

Thus, his schedule would contain more than just a list of activities and projects. It would reflect decisions to build certain relationships and priorities…and put others on hold. He also managed time to cultivate his own soul. For him, that meant writing over a thousand songs that regularly allowed him time to weep and time to laugh.

Solomon teaches us that time management is a matter of *wisdom* before it is a matter of *scheduling*. It deals with what is appropriate to do, or be, or feel right now, given what is happening in my life, by God's providence. We must use our time to manage the things that currently matter *most*. We must acknowledge what God is doing in our lives and respond to the way things actually are, instead of the way we wish they were.

Changing Seasons

I would like to draw two implications out of this profound insight of Solomon's. First, our priorities need to change as our life situation changes. Solomon experienced and accomplished so much in his lifetime, but he did not do it all at once. Solomon paced himself over 40 years of rule. As a young man, he personally attended to judgments rendered to commoners. It can't have been too common for a king to decide between two prostitutes. But Solomon wanted to understand the judicial system and the needs of his people, and he wanted to set the standards for justice early on. Later, as he got to know the bureaucracy and appointed key personnel, Scripture records how he formed a leadership team for the nation that would build the best infrastructure the nation would ever know. And all the while, Solomon kept writing proverbs and songs to keep his soul supple.

When Solomon thought of time management, he thought in terms of a lifetime. "What is appropriate for me to be doing and feeling at this point in my life? Which relationships should I be emphasizing and cultivating at this time?"

Life has its seasons. Understanding them is the key to being stewards of our time. Yet, when we think of time management, we often think only in terms of a daily schedule. We get into ruts, thinking that every day and every year should be the same. Some people decide on a set of life priorities and freeze them forever. Others pretend that everything is equally important, all the time. Such static thinkers are so clueless, or so busy, that their souls often burn out long before their bodies get around to dying. And they will miss half of the beauty this life can offer.

We need a lifetime view of time management. What should I be building in this season of my life? What should I concentrate on tearing down? What relationships do I need to focus on in these years? What feelings should I cultivate; what emotions should I be exploring? Sweet or sour? The honey of laughter or the bitterness of tears? How should I be responding to God's providences right now?

Think about the things of eternal value that will follow you into eternity. Your body, God's temple on earth, destined to be raised incorruptible. Your mind that can enable you to make your whole life a living sacrifice of praise. Your children, your neighbor, your planet and its creatures, your church. God has allotted to you a certain amount of time to cultivate and manage these things. Your time in this world is a disposable tool to use in managing these things of eternal value.

What season of life are you in right now? It is not the same season as those that came before; neither will this season last forever. Are you stuck in a rut, determined to give to your job or your family or your church the same amount of attention you've always given those things? Are you willing to adapt to the season? Are you willing to cut back whatever needs to be cut back, in order to embrace and build up a relationship that should be built up right now? Or, are you willing to invest more outside of the relationships that nurture you because your larger stewardship to your neighbor, your world or your church demands it? Are you willing to tear your clothes, sit in the dust and weep for a while because of what has happened to you or the people you care about? Or, are you willing to invest in a celebration to mark something that's just too good to let slip by unnoticed?

In each season of life, the Lord is waiting to meet you as you respond appropriately, in faith. Ignore the season, just let external demands automatically fill your schedule, and you will miss an appointment with God that could have made your life immensely rich.

Facing Tough Times

Another implication of Solomon's approach is the realization that we need to stop hiding from the negative and difficult things that happen to us. Of course, I'm not saying that we should let negative situations develop, if we can help it. But when we find ourselves unavoidably in a season of life that calls for difficult or sorrowful response, then that is what we must choose. "There is a time for everything." Just after our text, Solomon wrote, "He has made everything beautiful in its time." God will work for the good of those who love Him…in *everything*. Every situation in life, even the negative ones, can be made beautiful in its season. We need to recognize the season and live accordingly, so we can appreciate the beauty that God can bring out of the trials and sorrows of this fallen and ruined world.

For example, "there is…a time to mourn." Mourning is not a bad thing when it is time to mourn. There are dear Christians who are unable to mourn because they believe it demonstrates a lack of faith. But there is nothing wrong with seeking comfort and support when part of your life is ripped away. It is wrong to mourn too long, it is wrong to mourn too early, and for the Christian, it is wrong to mourn without hope. But when it is time to mourn, then we should mourn the loss of loved ones, or loss of our career. We should mourn a broken relationship or a broken body. Proper mourning is a beautiful thing. It testifies to the worth of what we have lost, and how much it meant to us. It naturally brings forth gratitude and praise to God for what He has given. It brings to mind the hope that we have in Christ, and stimulates our anticipation of the day when all death will be swallowed up in victory.

"There is a time...to throw away." We keep old memories and old insights like treasured heirlooms. But sometimes, they can be nothing more than mummified pain. Dwelling on them, allowing them to govern our present can be a very bad thing. The same Lord, who says, "Remember the former things, those of long ago" (Isaiah 46:9) can, when such memories hinder the present, say, "Forget the former things; do not dwell on the past. See, I am doing a new thing! Now it springs up; do you not perceive it?" (Isaiah 43:18-19) When the former things chain us to the past, they need to be thrown away. Negative memories and convictions can be difficult to dislodge; they provide a sense of security by giving us some kind of roots. But Solomon says that there comes a time when some things need to be uprooted. Throwing away security blankets that keep our faith infantile can be very painful. But if done at the right time, such putting away of childish things will help us grow up in our faith. And that will make our lives far more beautiful.

"There is...a time to hate." We should never love evil; we should hate it. When we see injustice and pain and oppression and ignorance and foolishness, it is time to hate. Not people—only God has the right to hate people. We must, rather, hate the conditions that sap the humanity out of those created in God's image. We should hate those situations and fight to change them. That is how God's beauty is often forged in this world.

The truth is that in this world, "There is a time for everything, and a season for every activity under heaven." And the good news is that, in Christ, "[God] has made everything beautiful in its time." We can know that beauty. We can watch God turn negative things to our good, if we will love Him and trust in His love.

Perhaps today, Solomon can teach us to stop ignoring some negative thing that God Almighty, our Heavenly Father, has allowed to touch us. If it is a negative thing, then it is not to be celebrated. Indeed, it may be sent by your enemy, the Evil One. But God has *promised* to work for your good until Christ returns, even in the midst of pain and loss and sorrow, if you will stop ignoring and running from this season of your life, and meet Him there.

Christian, is this a time for war? Is God calling you to justly oppose evil in this world with force? Has He called you or someone you dearly love to go into harm's way? Then set about finding God in wartime. Learn to put aside self-righteousness and focus on what is truly righteous and worthy. Learn to put aside personal or racial hatred, and focus your hate on malicious violence and ignorance and intolerable oppression. When it is time for war, pray that God will bring something noble and enduring and beautiful out of it.

Christian, is this a time for you to refrain from embracing? If you are without a spouse, is God calling you to focus your energies on raising your children single-handedly, or accomplishing good in this world and in His church with single-minded devotion? Or is this a time for Him to mold you and heal you, and shake off the sin that clings to you so closely, so that you will be a good spouse to someone He is preparing for you? If singleness is your season of life, then set about finding God in your singleness. Learn to put aside self-pity and cast your genuine cares on the One who cares for you. Learn to focus your energies in ways that please Him. If it is a time for singleness, look for the beauty God will bring out of this season of your life.

And Christian, for all of us, there will be a time to die. While many of us do not see it coming, many others of us will have a season to prepare for death. When that season arrives, let's set about exalting the Lord in whom we trust. Let's learn to put our fear of the unknown into perspective, the huge perspective of eternal life in Jesus Christ. May our last hours here be our finest hours here. May our faith in Christ bloom and blossom as never before. When it is time to die, pray that God would make it the most beautiful season of all.

At Christ's return, we will not be placing time before Him as an offering, for our years here were never more than a throwaway tool. But the best gifts will be given by those who have spent the most time walking with Him, adapting their priorities to the season. To such servants, He will say, "In every season, I waited to meet you at the appropriate place. And you were always careful to come and find me. We accomplished a great deal together that way. In eternity, every day will be even more precious, so won't you lead the way in seeking my will?"

Prayer

Father, we realize that all the seasons of this life have been sanctified and are appropriate for your blessing. You know all about giving your blessing at just the right times. In the fullness of time, you sent your Son. In the fullness of time, He died for our sins and rose again. In the fullness of time, you sent your Spirit to open our eyes and bring us to life.

So we each ask you Lord, "What time is it now? What do we need to focus on now, and what do we need to lay aside?" Lord, lift us above our well worn ruts, to see our situation, exercise our emotions and make decisions appropriate to this season of life.

And help us as well, Holy Father, to see our entire lives as but one season that will soon transition into another. Give us an eternal perspective that will help us make the most of each day. We pray in Jesus' name. Amen.

Questions for Discussion

Ecclesiastes 3:1-8

Look at each pair of seasons listed.

Paraphrase each line. What does each season really involve?
Which are the seasons with which you have had the least personal experience? Do you think you will experience them sometime in the future?

"There is a season for every activity under heaven"

There are problems living in the winter as if it were the summer and vice-versa. Can you think of some typical problems that arise when people refuse to address the season of life they are in, and pretend they are living in a different season?

"There is a time for everything"

If this is true, then do we have to rethink the common feeling that we "just don't have enough time."
How much time do we need? In general terms, what is it that we need time to accomplish? (cf. Matthew 6:10)

Specifically, consider how we are currently using our time to attend to:

the care of our bodies
the cultivation of our minds
the raising of our children/next generation
the needs of our neighbor
the welfare of the Earth
the growth of the Church

Should any of the above aspects of our stewardship receive greater or lesser attention in different seasons of life?

If so, how does that affect the planning of our *life*time?

The Life That Is Truly Life

○ ○

Command those who are rich in this present world not to be arrogant nor to put their hope in wealth, which is so uncertain, but to put their hope in God, who richly provides us with everything for our enjoyment. Command them to do good, to be rich in good deeds, and to be generous and willing to share. In this way they will lay up treasure for themselves as a firm foundation for the coming age, so that they may take hold of the life that is truly life.

—1 Timothy 6:17-19

Stewardship is finding joy in managing what God gives us for His glory. In this life, we look after a number of things of eternal value. God has also given us tools with which to manage the really important treasures. There is a difference between something you prepare as a gift, and the tools you use to prepare it. The gift, you give as an act of love. The tools are necessary, but when the time comes to give your gift, you lay the tools aside. Our time in this world, our money and our spiritual gifts are all temporary tools to help us manage the really important things.

In our text, Paul tells Timothy to address those in the church who are rich. Most of us would probably say at this point, "Well, that let's me out." Few of us consider ourselves rich. We think, rather, of the lifestyles of the rich and famous, or the many TV programs which are set in fabulously wealthy environments. We get the impression that our humble abode and several-year-old car put us out of the rich category.

Certainly, there is a level of "fabulously wealthy" which is way over our heads, but "rich" does not mean fabulously wealthy. Especially when the ancient church was made up of so many poor people, and even slaves, the wealthy were simply property holders with disposable income. We take it for granted that we have some disposable income—never as much as we would like, no doubt. But the fact is, that we are the wealthiest large society in history. Each person in this room is wealthy compared to most people alive today. I think that for the purposes of this text, if you and I have disposable income, then we may consider ourselves rich. We have money for our basic needs, and to spare.

Money Addiction

"Command those who are rich in this present world not to be arrogant nor to put their hope in wealth, which is so uncertain." Some look at passages like this one and think the Bible has a negative attitude toward wealth itself. That is not really true. Many famous biblical characters were wealthy, and their wealth did not hamper their spirituality. "O LORD…you still the hunger of those you cherish; their sons have plenty, and they store up wealth for their children." (Psalm 17:14) Wisdom cries out, "I walk in the way of righteousness, along the paths of justice, bestowing wealth on those who love me and making their treasuries full." (Proverbs 8:20-21) "The blessing of the LORD brings wealth, and he adds no trouble to it." (Proverbs 10:22)

The problem with wealth is that it is so easy to use it like a drug. Drugs are powerful medicine; they can do great good and relieve symptoms of pain. But drugs can become addictive. When we focus only on relieving the symptoms of pain and ignore the source of pain—not only physical discomfort, but emotional pain—we become dependent on the drug to keep us going. The drug actually works to mask the underlying disease or dysfunction. Similarly, wealth is a gift of God, given to enable us to meet many needs in life. It's a gift from God. "Remember the LORD your God, for it is he who gives you the ability to produce wealth." (Deuteronomy 8:18) But when we focus on money itself, we forget that it is *God* who provides for our needs, not the money. That's when, Paul says, we become arrogant, and put our hope in money instead of the Lord.

Just before our text, Paul said, "People who want to get rich fall into temptation and a trap and into many foolish and harmful desires that plunge men into ruin and destruction. For the love of money is a root of all kinds of evil. Some people, eager for money, have wandered from the faith and pierced themselves with many griefs." (1 Timothy 6:9-10) To have or produce wealth is a gift of God to help us meet needs. But to focus on wealth itself, to want to get rich, is to use money as a drug. Such a desire is a trap that plunges people into ruin and destruction. It is not money, then, but the *love* of money, the focus on money and wealth, that is a root of all kinds of evil. Relying on money instead of the Lord for happiness will lure you away from faith in God, so that your life will be pierced with many griefs.

Everyone who is wealthy is subject to the temptation to use money as a drug. I know that 95% of us are thinking, "I have no problem holding my wealth," just as so many say, "I have no problem holding my liquor. O, don't worry, I can handle alcohol, or nicotine, or some other drug—I'm in control!" Friend, if you have a cavalier attitude about the temptation to rely on your money instead of on the Lord, you may be just fooling yourself. Money is meant to be a tool, but it is easier than you think to allow it to become your master.

Jesus once said, "No one can serve two masters. Either he will hate the one and love the other, or he will be devoted to the one and despise the other. You cannot serve both God and Money." (Matthew 6:24) Jesus went on to describe how we can tell if money is our master. The one who has the Lord as His master trusts that God knows his needs, and *rests* in the confidence that God will provide for Him. The one with the Lord as his master will seek first God's kingdom and trust that the stuff he needs will be given to him. In contrast, the one who trusts in his own wealth will *worry* about what will become of him. He will be obsessed with fretting about his needs and his future, unsure if he has enough money to meet his needs.

Poor believers must battle depression and envy, but rich believers must endure the constant, powerful temptation to hope in their wealth. No wonder a wise man once said, "give me neither poverty nor riches, but give me only my daily bread. Otherwise, I may have too much and disown you and say, 'Who is the LORD?' Or I may become poor and steal, and so dishonor the name of my God." (Proverbs 30:8-9) To be poor means that you and your family do not eat regularly. To be rich means that you are accustomed to having more than you need. There are temptations either way.

If we depend on the things we can buy to make us happy, they will pull us away from God. If we let it, money will act as a drug to rob us of vitality. Drugs rarely, if ever, actually heighten awareness and ability. They often give us that impression, but it's an illusion. For example, many people think of alcohol as a stimulant, but taken internally, it depresses the body's function. It feels like a stimulant because it suppresses our moral awareness. When you abuse a drug, it gives the illusion of happiness, but actually strips away part of your ability to be happy.

I can't stand taking certain cold medications. They put me in a stupor—sure, I don't notice the body ache of a cold, but I don't notice much else, either. I feel like I'm under water, moving slowly. I don't want to stay there. I want to get it out of my system and get my life back. We don't want money to become a drug that drains our life away.

It doesn't have to.

Waking Up to Life

"Command those who are rich in this present world…to put their hope in God, who richly provides us with everything for our enjoyment. Command them to do good, to be rich in good deeds, and to be generous and willing to share. In this way they…may take hold of the life that is truly life." *The life that is truly life*…what an exciting phrase to find in a passage about money! Is it possible that you and I, as wealthy Christians, barely know what it really means to be alive? There are poor, miserable babies who are born addicted to alcohol, caffeine, nicotine, or even opiates like heroin, because their mothers were addicted. Those kids cannot even begin to know what it properly means to be alive until they go through withdrawal. For them, life is hazed over until they become free of the drug.

If we look at it spiritually, we *all* were born hooked on sin in many ways. Until the power of sin is broken, we cannot taste what it really means to be spiritually alive. Paul once said that a new believer comes to see Christ and all others differently after conversion (cf. 2 Corinthians 5:16) But he also said that what believers are able to see is, at first, no more than "a poor reflection in a mirror" (cf. 1 Corinthians 13:12); it's hazy, like looking underwater. As our faith grows, the image begins to clear up. When Christ returns and we see Him face to face, we will see all things clearly. Until then, the haze lifts to the degree that we get sin out of our system. Trusting in our money and misusing it keeps us in the haze of sin.

The great thing is that properly using our money can help to bring us out of the haze. Jesus said, "Provide purses for yourselves that will not wear out, a treasure in heaven that will not be exhausted, where no thief comes near and no moth destroys. For where your treasure is, there your heart will be also." (Luke 12:33-34) We can use our treasure to build up our souls.

Paul says this, and more, in our text. He encourages us to purposefully use the wealth we have as a tool of our stewardship. Then he declares, "In this way they…[we] may take hold of the life that is truly life." The life of the coming age, when God's will is finally done on earth as it is in heaven, the life we will finally enjoy when sin is finally purged from our system, is life that is truly life. Paul is teaching that we can take hold of that life *now* through the way we use our wealth.

What an amazing claim! We can actually experience something of the joys of paradise now, by properly using money as a tool in our stewardship. How's that for a positive view of wealth! While it is death to look to money for our happiness, happiness is exactly what we will find when we use our wealth as a tool to manage other things of eternal value. "The life that is truly life" has utter confidence that God will provide, so it is able to use money as a tool to share the blessings God has already given us.

Most people have no idea that life is meant to be such a joyful dependence upon God. We are born into this world desperate to provide for our own happiness. Sin twisted our soul, so that we do not trust God. We do not believe He is truly good. We do not believe He truly has our best interests at heart. That was the fundamental temptation in the Garden of Eden, and we bought it. And ever since, we have been trapped in a miserable view that God is someone we cannot trust to care for us. No, we must care for ourselves, by accumulating and trusting in our own wealth. As long as we remain trapped in that lie, we can never be fully alive. The life we do experience is doomed to be empty, full of fear and anxiety. We place our hope in the efficiency of own selfishness.

Jesus, and Jesus alone, frees us from such sin. His cross *proves* that God has our best interests at heart. It proves that God not only loves us, but that He is a good, generous and worthy friend. Jesus demonstrates that the Living God who made all things loves to give. He made the universe to share the beauty of His mind openly. He created mankind in His image so that we could share His goodness, and imitate Him by sharing it with each other. Our sin wrecked all that, but God's grace is overcoming our sin.

One day, God's people shall know what it means to live the life God designed. One day, our spirit will be clear—no haze, no fog. We'll see our God for the magnificent Being He is, who makes the heart swell just to think of Him, who makes us want to give ourselves wholly as a living sacrifice for the sheer joy of being like Him. We'll leave the underwater haze of sin behind, and we will know "the life that is truly life."

But look at this! The Apostle Paul says that we can begin to take hold of that life *now*, as we exercise our faith. Today, we can taste the life that shall be ours forever. And one of the key ways we can do this is so *simple*: just use our discretionary income to share the blessings we already have.

"Command those who are rich in this present world…to do good, to be rich in good deeds, and to be generous and willing to share." The word "rich" is used twice: once for monetary wealth, and once for the accomplishment of good, literally *beautiful*, deeds. Paul says we take hold of true life by translating the one kind of wealth into the other.

Life-in-a-fog, the dull, half-awake, half-conscious life most people know, life that sees God as either dead or uncaring, or even as an enemy—that kind of life uses wealth in the desperate attempt to make *me* more beautiful. Get all the options and accessories I can. Such things can be blessings, but when they are all I have, they are pathetic. They testify to a life so devoid of meaning, it needs stuff in bulk to give it a sense of importance. It is so devoid of beauty, it needs to hide behind beautiful things to temper its ugliness.

Life that is truly life finds happiness in using wealth to accomplish God's beautiful will in this world and in this life. The more we work with God to share His blessing, the more filled with meaning our own lives become. The more we give away, the clearer we can see who we are. And who we are is beautiful, because we're starting to look like Him. To be rich in beautiful deeds is to be generous and ready to give. Joyful Christians are those who are ready to imitate God in creative, overflowing good will. Ready to use disposable income as a steward, caring for the things of eternal value God has given to me. To be rich in beautiful deeds is to be ready to share.

What Money Could Buy

"Ready to share" is the same root word as *koinonia*, or fellowship. Joyful Christians are especially ready to share their money easily with other Christians. "All the believers were one in heart and mind. No one claimed that any of his possessions was his own, but they shared everything they had. With great power the apostles continued to testify to the resurrection of the Lord Jesus, and much grace was upon them all. There were no needy persons among them. For from time to time those who owned lands or houses sold them, brought the money from the sales and put it at the apostles' feet, and it was distributed to anyone as he had need." (Acts 4:32-35) I've heard so many commentators try to explain how this profound level of mutual care is not mandatory, maybe not even wise. OK, maybe it isn't mandatory, but I wish I had more of that spirit. With such a spirit, financial sharing is not a chore; it's a joy—the joy of making sure everyone shares God's blessings to the full.

According to Jesus, stewardship of money is not just about the impact our sharing has on others. It's about the impact on *our* lives, too, as we discover what life is truly all about. When He told the parable of the rich fool, He said, "a man's life does not consist in the abundance of his possessions." (Luke 12:15) Several times, He said that life is more than food and clothing—all the stuff you can buy with money. Jesus spoke of eternal life not only as everlasting life, but as a quality of life that can only be experienced by someone who truly knows the good God who made us.

If you truly know the God who made all this beautiful universe just because He wanted to, who rested after creation but then went back to work after our sin to redeem a multitude, who sent His only beloved Son to die in order that we might live…if you know that God, then you will understand and affirm the words of the Lord Jesus, quoted by Paul, "It is more blessed to give than to receive." (Acts 20:33)

The context of that quote is money. Paul used that phrase to summarize the lifestyle he cherished and enjoyed. Jesus had set him free to lose his old life and find a new one. Money was no longer his master. It became a tool to help him steward the gifts of lasting value God had entrusted to him. Can you imagine living a life that truly believed that it is more blessed, it makes me *happier*, to use money to accomplish beautiful things, than it is to receive money to spend on my own vanity?

How can we become better stewards of the money God has given us? Ultimately, the answer is not found in tweaking budgets a little and sacrificing small offerings in order to protect the rest of my income from God's greedy little hands. The answer is found in embracing God for who He is. He is the wonderful Lord who not only owns the cattle on a thousand hills, but who is richer beyond measure in good deeds. He is the God who is willing and happy to give anything He has, even His own Son, to accomplish something beautiful in the likes of you and me.

I know that I am becoming a good steward of my disposable income when I find myself growing wealthy in good deeds that care for the things of eternal value that God has entrusted to me.

Good deeds such as using my money to care for myself. Providing good food, good shelter, good clothing, all the needs of life to enhance the body God has entrusted to me. Providing for my mind, my soul, in terms of godly opportunities for growth and recreation. "God…richly provides us with everything for our enjoyment." I am a good steward when I enjoy how God is taking care of me, because that is what God gave me money for.

Good deeds such as putting my money to work taking care of my children. Providing for their physical and intellectual and emotional needs. Investing in education and camps and missions projects and whatever will help them to grow in godliness, because that is what God gave me money for.

Good deeds such as investing my money in caring for neighbors, near or far. Helping a family I know that has fallen into disaster. Showing mercy to families I may not know, with a loaf of bread or a bit of simple medicine that will restore a child dying from diarrhea. Supplying dignity by supporting a fledgling third world business through my Christmas shopping. Helping whole people groups and refugee movements experiencing wholesale disaster, because that is what God gave me money for.

Good deeds such as caring for the planet and its creatures, the creatures God entrusted to our care a long time ago. Yes, we can eat them and use them, but we were also charged to care for them and enhance their existence in this world. I can do that on a local scale, watching over local strays and local land development, or I get involved on a larger scale, because that is what God gave me money for.

Good deeds such as sharing my money with fellow believers, caring for them when they are in need. And providing support for those who are lonely, or worn out, or in need of recovery, or who have a great ministry they want to develop. Not to mention sending out dozens of men and women ready to take the gospel to places currently ignorant of it. That is what God gave me money for.

Christian, one day, you will stand before your Creator to give an account of your stewardship. When it comes time for you to lay your gifts before Him, you won't be laying out your financial statements. He won't want to see your tools; He'll want to see what you did with them. To you, God entrusted your body, mind, children, neighbor, planet and the church. He also gave you some money as a tool, a resource, to manage it all. From some of us, He will receive a wealth of good, beautiful deeds: grateful care for oneself, loving care for our children, generous care for neighbors, responsible care for the planet, faithful and enthusiastic care for His church. "You really enjoyed using that money, didn't you? You enjoyed living like...Me. Accomplishing beautiful things seems to be your idea of being alive. Well, that's my idea, too! Look, I'm going to make a society more free, more full of beauty than anyone has ever imagined. I want to build it with people like you. I've seen what you can do with a little; let's see what you can do with a lot!"

Prayer

Heavenly Father, have mercy on us. Our lives are fogged up by self-dependence and pride. We are spiritually alive, but some of us barely so. Our appetite for happiness is so weak and sickly that we think it can be filled by things and the envy they stimulate in others. We fear that we will go through our entire lives here afraid to give, afraid to share, afraid to really live, and that we will only realize what we have been missing when we get to heaven.

Lord, we would like to embrace life to the full right now. We would take hold of the life that is truly life, the life that consists of more than the abundance of our possessions, the life that finds more blessing in giving than receiving, the life that will leave this world and its money behind one day, only to find itself rich in good deeds, stored up in heaven where we will present them to you.

Thank you for desiring us to be like you—as free, as giving, as creatively good at making good things happen. We can't wait to get started. In fact, by your grace, we won't wait to get started. We'll get started right now, in Christ's name. Amen.

Questions for Discussion

1 Timothy 6:17-19

What are some inherent dangers or temptations in being wealthy?

What difference is there between putting one's hope in wealth, and putting one's hope in God?

Why does God give us what He gives us?

Paul speaks of "life that is truly life"

How is life dulled when money is used like a drug?
How does life "come alive" when we use money to become "rich in good deeds"?

What do you think it means to "lay up treasure for the coming age"? (cf. Luke 12:15-34)

Faithfully Administering God's Grace

o o o o o o o o o o o o o o o o o o o o o o o o o o o o o o o o o

The end of all things is near. Therefore be clear minded and self-controlled so that you can pray. Above all, love each other deeply, because love covers over a multitude of sins. Offer hospitality to one another without grumbling. Each one should use whatever gift he has received to serve others, faithfully administering God's grace in its various forms. If anyone speaks, he should do it as one speaking the very words of God. If anyone serves, he should do it with the strength God provides, so that in all things God may be praised through Jesus Christ. To him be the glory and the power for ever and ever. Amen.

—1 Peter 4:7-11

Stewardship is joyfully managing what God has given us for His glory. On the day of judgment, the Lord will evaluate the effort and the joy we devoted to managing what He gave us in this life. This evaluation has no bearing on our salvation, but it has everything to do with our opportunities for service in paradise. God has given us many things that will follow us into eternity: our bodies, minds, children, neighbors, our planet and the church. These are the things we must manage; they are like gifts we are preparing to lay before Him. We are also given tools with which to prepare these gifts, resources more or less tied to this life, such as our life span in this world and our money. We will not take these resources with us, but we need them now, as tools of our stewardship. One tool left to consider is our spiritual gifts. Of all the tools we have, these are most explicitly associated in Scripture with our stewardship, as illustrated in the text quoted above.

Understanding Spiritual Gifts

Spiritual gifts are a mystery to a great many Christians. Most of us have heard of spiritual gifts, but we're not sure what they are, and the large majority of believers have no idea how they are gifted. Many Christians only know about spiritual gifts because of the modern Charismatic movement. The word translated "spiritual gift" is the Greek word *charismata*. *Charis* is the word for grace, *charismata* is an instance, or manifestation of grace. While the word is often translated in the Bible simply as "gift" for the lack of any other elegant option, we must remember that the meaning of the word has to do with the way God manifests His grace.

Some of the ancient spiritual gifts seem strange to us today, such as the gift of tongues, or the gift of super-strength (Samson), although they made perfect sense at the time. But there are many more permanent examples of God's grace in church. The Book of Romans tells us that spiritual gifts include serving, teaching, encouraging, financial empowerment, leadership and mercy. The Old Testament adds artistic skill, music and wisdom. Every list of gifts is different; we aren't given a definitive number to work with because there are many ways that God's grace is manifested.

Spiritual gifts are different from our general loving demeanor toward one another. Note how Peter talks about Christian virtue in general. "The end of all things is near. Therefore be clear-minded and self-controlled so that you can pray. Above all, love each other deeply, because love covers over a multitude of sins. Offer hospitality to one another without grumbling." Normal Christian behavior includes self-control, prayer and hospitality.

Spiritual gifts, on the other hand, vary from Christian to Christian, as we are entrusted with different abilities that bring God's blessing to others. The Holy Spirit "gives [gifts] to each one, just as he determines." (1 Corinthians 12:11) The Holy Spirit chooses to give each of us a different aspect of God's grace to deliver. In other words, they are gifts that do not belong to us; we are entrusted with them to deliver to others.

Peter doesn't even try to give us a list of spiritual gifts. He just says that they come in various forms. The underlying Greek suggests a many-colored spectrum. Peter does, however, put them in two categories.

"If anyone speaks, he should do it as one speaking the very words of God." Sometimes, we need God's grace in verbal form, as in encouragement, teaching, comfort, exhortation, preaching or wise counsel. Anyone can speak with love; anyone can use the Scriptures to speak the truth. But some of us are gifted by the Holy Spirit to pass on God's grace with our words. It's God's grace and God's words, but the Holy Spirit gives us power to encourage, impart wisdom, lift up, explain, expose, warn and proclaim the gospel. God's grace is most powerfully *heard* when those gifted people use their gifts.

"If anyone serves, he should do it with the strength God provides." Sometimes, we need God's grace in the form of action, not words. We need deeds, from hands-on mercy to high-level administration. Anyone can perform acts of kindness, or lead a ministry program. But some of us are gifted by the Holy Spirit to be more effective in passing on God's grace with our deeds. The Holy Spirit gives us power to express God's love and accomplish His work through practical action. This could involve anything from organization, to financial administration, to decorating, to visiting a hurting soul. God's grace is most powerfully *seen* when those who are gifted use their gifts.

Special Deliveries

Spiritual gifts are a principal aspect of our stewardship. "Each one should use whatever gift he has received to serve others, faithfully administering God's grace in its various forms." *Administering* is the biblical word for stewardship. So Peter plainly states that all of us are stewards of one or more spiritual gifts, through which we manage God's grace to one another.

I found this text to be life-changing, for it explained to me how I receive the grace of God. I receive it through you.

Think about this carefully. Christian, how do you receive God's grace? How do you receive encouragement, wisdom, help, mercy, healing? How do these practical experiences of God's grace come into your life? Of course, God is the source of all grace. All grace is grounded in Christ's work and is sent to us by the Holy Spirit. But did you appreciate that *we* are the ones who manage the final delivery of God's grace to each other?

Consider this verse again, "Each one should use whatever gift he has received to serve others, faithfully administering God's grace in its various forms." *We* administer, or manage God's grace for each other. It's sent from God, paid for by Christ and transported via air freight by the Holy Spirit to be unloaded right at your door. But the grace shipped to you doesn't have your name on it! It's got the names of other people on it, because you are the last link in the delivery. Spiritual gifts describe the way you and I administer God's grace to one another. God's grace rarely comes to us directly; it usually comes through another believer. Did you know that?

Day by day, when we pick up our mail from God, we find lots of wonderful opportunities to be a good steward of our minds, bodies, neighbors, children, planet and church. "I think I'll give some time to this, today," or "I think I'll invest some money in this." But occasionally, we find in our mail from God, packages of grace—potent, life-changing grace—that have other people's names on it. Maybe an individual's name, or maybe a group's name like "to the children of the church" or "to single moms," or "to an adult Sunday School class," or "to the homeless of Baltimore." Is all this mail misaddressed? No, God simply wants you to deliver these packages of His grace personally.

That's what spiritual gifts are all about. The kinds of packages God entrusts us to deliver are different for each of us. God sends each one to those especially equipped to deliver them. We notice that we tend to receive the same sort of packages on a regular basis. Some receive words of grace to speak to others because they have a speaking gift. Some receive deeds of love to perform for others because they have a particular doing gift. We can all say and do godly things for one another. But the Holy Spirit has chosen to give each of us especially potent, effective, powerful packages of God's grace to deliver for Him. The nature of the packages you receive corresponds to your spiritual gift.

Why does God do this? Because God intended for you and me to be in His image. As we grow in Christ, God wants us to love others powerfully, as He does. So He allows us to handle one little aspect of His power. Maybe more, but at least one. He won't overload any of us, but He will give each of His children some special manifestation of His grace and love to deliver in His name. When you deliver it, the Holy Spirit makes it come alive; He gives it power. You get to see God work before your eyes, and you get to be a part of it. It's as if Jesus were present at that moment, ministering *through you*. That is what *charismata*, spiritual gifts are. They are real-time manifestations of God's grace running through your lips and fingers.

In your mailbox, you keep getting these packages of organization and structure addressed to various ministries in the church, because God has gifted you to bring *His* organization and structure to those ministries. Or you keep getting powerful words of comfort that others need—brothers and sisters who have lost their jobs, or lost a baby—because God has gifted you to bring *His* words of comfort to their pain. Or you keep getting money that other Christians need, or the church needs, so you can invest *His* funds to make a crucial difference. (I keep getting these sermons to deliver. I get one in my box every week!)

You don't find your spiritual gift by having somebody lay hands on you. I also doubt many discover their gifts through a survey. How, then, do know your spiritual gifts?

You discover your spiritual gifts by seeing how God enables you to deliver His blessing to others. You find your *charismata* by observing how God uses you to manifest His grace. You'll see it when people light up with insight, or open up to receive comfort, or rev up to accomplish their full potential—all through the power of God that the Holy Spirit delivers through you when you are faithful, "so that in all things God may be praised through Jesus Christ." That covers a lot of possibilities. Your gifts could include anything from leading a Bible study to baking pies. When we administer to others the grace He has entrusted to us, we are exercising spiritual gifts.

I Think I Have Something for You

When you and I think of "stewardship," we usually think of something personal, maybe even private. But spiritual gifts emphasize another dimension of our stewardship, a corporate dimension. We were never meant to manage the planet, or the needs of our neighbors, or raise our children, or even care for our own well being *alone*. We were meant to do it together. God's power to do these things is distributed among us, and we only experience His power fully when we work together.

"The body is a unit, though it is made up of many parts; and though all its parts are many, they form one body. So it is with Christ." (1 Corinthians 12:12) Paul develops his analogy carefully. Each member of the body needs all the others; the eye needs the hand and the head needs the feet. Each part of the body has something the other parts need. I cannot see without you and you cannot move without me. Paul says that the Holy Spirit gives manifestations of God's grace, or spiritual gifts, "to each one, just as he determines" and that he does so "for the common good." (1 Corinthians 12:11,7)

That means, Christian, that some of God's most powerful gifts of grace to the rest of us are in *your* possession. Personally, it means that God's most powerful gifts of grace to me may be in your possession, and some of His most powerful gifts to you may be in my possession. To the degree that we are faithful as stewards to administer and deliver our spiritual gifts, to that degree God's grace is made real and concrete in this world. To the degree that we do not, or will not administer His grace, to that degree I never receive it and you never receive it in this world. It came all the way from heaven to our doorstep, but was never delivered the rest of way.

Can you imagine *not* delivering a gift entrusted to you by God? Occasionally, someone comes up to me with an envelope, sometimes a check, sometimes cash. "I missed the offering, would you please see that this gets into today's offering?" How would they feel if I absent-mindedly tossed it under the pulpit, or in a drawer, and it just lay there—someone's gift of love to God, ignored, buried, forgotten? They would be disappointed, maybe even angry.

Micki and I do a lot of ordering over the internet. The UPS driver knows us well, and we also get boxes from the postman and Fed Ex. We often hear a *thump* outside the door as a package or two are delivered. Occasionally, we get something with a neighbor's name on it when he wasn't home to receive it. Are we not responsible to walk over and deliver that package? If a neighbor got one of our packages, should they not walk over and give it to us? How would we feel if we found out two months later that one of our neighbors just tossed our package into a corner and forgot about it?

Books and plays and movies have been made about letters that, for one reason or another, were delivered years after they were sent, and how whole lives were affected by the delay. How are lives affected when God's grace goes undelivered? Did you ever feel that God had abandoned you in a time of need? By His grace, you got over it; over time, the standard means of grace have been effective and healed your soul. But at the time, you really needed a powerful word of encouragement, or a simple act of love to remind you of God's love. And it wasn't there. Perhaps that was a day when one of us was a poor steward of the spiritual gift God entrusted us to deliver to you. We were too busy, too absorbed in getting ahead or licking our own wounds. We were too tired or too lazy. We've still got His gift for you, a very caring word, or an invitation to dinner—we've got it somewhere—maybe it's in the attic.

Today, there are needs in the church, plenty of them. People with chronic illness sigh under a lonely weight of pain. A tight budget puts needed equipment on hold. Children and teens trudge through a cultural quicksand threatening to suck them down, while programs for them stumble because there is no one to teach, or take care of organizational details, or lead in music. Single Moms wonder if God has forgotten them. It makes you wonder if some of us have stashed in the attic boxes and boxes of gifts from God, spiritual supplies needed by the Body of Christ, still undelivered.

God supplies all the grace His church needs, but we have to deliver it. I preach with some effectiveness simply because the Holy Spirit gives me sermons to deliver. But as for my management and counseling skills, my financial awareness, my hospitality, my understanding of children—there are hundreds of ways in which my ministry is just mediocre. Sure, I can do many of those things as well as the next person. And I should. But the Body of Christ can *shine* only when the people who are spiritually gifted deliver their gifts!

Christian, try to appreciate how important *your* spiritual gifts are. We often have this debilitating attitude that it is only the up-front gifts like music and preaching that really count in the church. If you think that way, you've got it all upside down. The up-front gifts are meant to inspire us to the *real* work of ministry, manifesting Jesus Christ to each other and to a world that needs Him. Do you really think that the heavenly record of how people received God's grace in Jesus Christ will be filled with sermon titles? Just think of how you have been touched by God's love in your life. Yes, sometimes, it has been through a sermon. But more often, it has been at a youth camp, or through an anonymous gift in a hard time, or an unexpected visit with prayer, or a Bible study someone hosted and someone else led. Or a homemade greeting card, or the simple gospel shared with you by a friend.

Christian, do you realize how valuable those boxes are, that have been delivered to your door? How much the rest of us need what you have been given to deliver to us? "The body is not made up of one part but of many...if the ear should say, 'Because I am not an eye, I do not belong to the body,' it would not for that reason cease to be part of the body. If the whole body were an eye, where would the sense of hearing be? If the whole body were an ear, where would the sense of smell be? But in fact God has arranged the parts in the body, every one of them, just as he wanted them to be. If they were all one part, where would the body be? As it is, there are many parts, but one body. The eye cannot say to the hand, 'I don't need you!' And the head cannot say to the feet, 'I don't need you!' On the contrary, those parts of the body that seem to be weaker are indispensable." (1 Corinthians 12:14-22)

Do you believe that? What God has given to you is *indispensable* to Christ's body! The way you set up the sound for a function could make all the difference as to whether a man ends up reopening his heart to his wife, instead of being distracted because he can't hear the testimony he needs to hear. Your creative writing could bring Scriptural truth to audiences who will never go to church. Your compassionate listening could be the one memory that, years later, brings tears to the eyes of a former child who thinks of you when she thinks of Christ. Your earnest music could make twice the impact of a sermon on the same theme, especially if you offer it in a hospital room or at a funeral. Your grasp of finances could multiply the impact of all the other spiritual gifts the church has.

I know that many of you have, indeed, been faithful in administering the grace of God entrusted to you. I can't wait to see you approach the Lord on the great Day of judgment, your sins covered, your future guaranteed, ready for your assignment in paradise. "Now, my beloved child. I have here a complete invoice of all the spiritual gifts I sent to your address. Let's see what you did with them...[Smile]...This is wonderful. Seems as though you *like* giving away my blessings. You know, I have a boatload of blessing to administer in paradise. I've got it all wrapped up and ready to go. I think I've found someone who will enjoy spending eternity delivering it!"

Prayer

When Peter spoke to us about our stewardship of your grace, he said, "the end of all things is near." Father, to our ears, that is not a threat, but a call to action.

Father, we need so much grace in this fallen world, so much grace. And we recognize, with Peter, that the grace we will receive in this world has been given us to manage for each other's benefit. It doesn't come directly out of the sky. We will receive it through each other.

Lord, we forgive our brothers and sisters who have withheld from us the grace you entrusted them to give us. And we look to them, and you, for similar forgiveness for our own laziness. But mostly, we are supremely thankful that you haven't stopped trusting us to pass on your love and your truth with power. We are delighted to have some part, to be some part of the Body of Christ. We will try not to envy the parts others have, because we are beginning to appreciate that each part is indispensable.

Father, multiply our joy as we pass on the spiritual gifts you have given us. We pray in Jesus' name.

Questions for Discussion

1 Peter 4:7-11

Paraphrase what it means to "administer God's grace."

When God gives you a manifestation of His grace, whom is it for? (That is, is it a gift intended for you, or intended for someone else?)

What are the "various forms" in which God's grace appears?

What are your spiritual gifts?

What makes you think so? or how can you find out?
How do you think God feels about any gifts He has entrusted to you, that you have not delivered?
How do you feel about the gifts God has for you, that others have not delivered?

How can we better encourage each other to administer the grace God entrusts to us for His church?

An Offering to the Lord

○ ○

In the course of time Cain brought some of the fruits of the soil as an offering to the LORD. But Abel brought fat portions from some of the firstborn of his flock. The LORD looked with favor on Abel and his offering, but on Cain and his offering he did not look with favor. So Cain was very angry, and his face was downcast. Then the LORD said to Cain, "Why are you angry? Why is your face downcast? If you do what is right, will you not be accepted? But if you do not do what is right, sin is crouching at your door; it desires to have you, but you must master it."

—*Genesis 4:3-7*

Stewardship is finding joy in managing the things God gives to us for His glory. We've looked at some of the things of eternal value that God has given us to manage, as well as the tools of time, money and spiritual gifts.

When people approach a study of biblical stewardship, however, they generally expect something on financial giving to the church. It is an emotionally charged subject, and one that is difficult for most pastors to address. Might there not be a conflict of interest when someone preaches about his own salary?

Well, if pastor's salaries were the issue, there might be a conflict of interest. But the theme I wish to address is not the relationship between religious offerings and a compensation package. We're going to look at the connection between offerings and worship. Our text in Genesis 4 takes us back to the very beginning of formal worship. The significance of this text tends to get lost because of the famous murder which occurs just afterwards. But today, our focus is the very first recorded religious offering.

The Genesis of Religion

When our first parents were created, there was no religion, just a covenant of life. God offered everlasting life to them if they would receive it in terms of steward-ship, ruling the earth to God's glory according to His character and His values. Originally, whatever worship there was, was offered every day in the way they managed the earth to God's glory. There was no formal religion in Eden because their stewardship made worship an all-the-time experience.

Sin changed all that. With sin, we exchanged God's glory for our glory as a motive for living, thus exchanging stewardship for pretended ownership. Pre-tending to own what God made took the worship out of everything we did; it ripped us away from the life God designed for us and left us to die outside of Eden. God revealed how He would save a portion of mankind through a prom-ised Savior. His salvation would bring people back to living for *His* glory, back to lives of total worship expressed through the stewardship of all we have and are.

Christians relearn this kind of worship through the formal religion given to us in the Bible. Formal religion uses rituals and symbols to teach the soul. When Christ returns, I don't know if we will even have formal worship services, since at that point we will have relearned how to worship God with our whole lives. But for now, we need to practice our worship.

Cain and Abel were children of Adam and Eve, and we assume that their parents taught them whatever they knew about formal worship. By the time of our text, they were old enough to practice their religion on their own. The text makes three important points about the religion they practiced.

First, it seems likely that they practiced their religion on the Sabbath. "In the course of time" Cain and Abel brought sacrifices. It is difficult to translate this Hebrew phrase. Literally, it means "at the end of the days." In other words, what is viewed here is a time interval. The time interval stressed in early Genesis is the week. It would seem, then, that religion was practiced at the end of the week. This would mean that worship was structured around the way God revealed His act of creation: six days of divine work paralleled by our dominion of this planet, and one day of divine rest paralleled by our worship. The Sabbath was the perfect day to regularly recognize our stewardship by symbolically dedicating the fruit of our dominion to God's glory.

The second thing we notice is that religion consisted of an offering. "In the course of time Cain brought some of the fruits of the soil as an offering to the LORD. But Abel brought fat portions from some of the firstborn of his flock." An offering is a physical gift to God, a tangible token of all our stewardship of the earth. We do not give God religious offerings because He needs them. He created all things; He certainly doesn't need what we can produce. We give tangible offerings to God to symbolize what worship is all about, our stewardship of everything for His glory. Religion practices worship by dedicating to God a portion of our labor, or the fruit of our labor, representing the ultimate devotion of all our life to Him.

What did they do with these offerings? How do you give something to God, even symbolically? You burn it up; you turn it into smoke and let it rise to heaven. This is how all the patriarchs worshiped. They built altars and burned their offerings. As Scripture would later put it, the offerings became a sweet aroma to God.

The key thing is to see how essential an offering is in formal worship, in human religion. We really don't know if this early worship included anything else at this point. Prayers? Recitation of God's words given to Adam? Singing? We have no idea. It seems as though the very essence of formal worship, when it began, was an offering, a tangible gift of one's substance, dedicated and sent to God in the flames. That *was* our religion: an offering to God made on the Sabbath day.

The third thing the text tells us, is that the physical offering was symbolic of an inner attitude. "The LORD looked with favor on Abel and his offering, but on Cain and his offering he did not look with favor." In other words, one offering was acceptable, and one was not. Some people have mistakenly assumed that what made Abel's offering acceptable had to do with what he offered, an animal instead of vegetables. But as you read on in the text, you see that God warned Cain that he was harboring sin in his heart, and it was ready to pounce on him if he didn't control it. That was why his offering was refused. This point is underscored in the New Testament, "By faith Abel offered God a better sacrifice than Cain did. By faith he was commended as a righteous man, when God spoke well of his offerings." (Hebrews 11:4) Abel did not depend on his offering to make him righteous in God's sight; Abel had faith in God's promises of a Savior, made to Adam and Eve. Abel's offering reflected a genuine, humble desire to offer himself to God out of gratitude and love, and that made his offering acceptable. Cain was contemplating how he could advance his own interests at his brother's expense, and you cannot worship God with such a self-justifying heart. Worship is an inner devotion to God's glory. Acceptable religion symbolizes true devotion through a physical offering.

What we learn from this text is that from the earliest days, formal worship consisted of presenting an offering of one's substance to God. This virtually defined Sabbath religion, at least by the second generation of the human race. This offering was tangible; it involved the fruit of one's labor. It was also symbolic, in that the offering was burned and symbolically sent to God. The whole point was to religiously illustrate an inner heart of worship, dedicating one's entire life to the glory of God.

Not Just a Collection

This text has the potential of turning our sentimental approach to formal worship on its head. Emotionally, we respond most to singing, or maybe a good sermon, or testimony or prayer. The offering is kind of a down time in our services. We try to spice it up with special music, or perhaps an impressive doxology. Why? Because today, we have largely replaced the notion of an offering with the notion of a collection, a collection of money to run the church. It is as if all we are doing in that part of the service is pooling our resources to keep the church going. But now we see that before there were any religious expenses to worry about, before there was any singing or preaching, maybe even before there was prayer, there was an offering. More than anything else, an offering demonstrates the stewardship of our lives. It is the essence of religion, expressing our commitment to manage all things for the glory of God.

Religious worship is best represented by the literal dedication of some of our things to His glory. We'll see how this offering got connected to supporting church expenses in a moment. But the surprising fact is that our offering would be quite proper and would lose nothing of its religious value if we brought it forward, sprinkled it with lighter fluid, and lit a match. When that image makes sense to you, the image of everything in the offering plate going up in smoke, then you will understand what a religious offering is. We tangibly give a portion of our income *to God*, to religiously practice the dedication of all the fruit of all our labor to God's glory.

Physical offerings of our substance have always been a central part of biblical religion. Much later, with Israel, God commanded, "Three times a year all your men must appear before the LORD your God at the place he will choose: at the Feast of Unleavened Bread, the Feast of Weeks and the Feast of Tabernacles. No man should appear before the LORD empty-handed." (Deuteronomy 16:16) That phrase summarizes the religious practice of our stewardship. *No man should appear before the Lord empty-handed.*

In the Old Testament, the formal worship of God was designed to be costly. Financial gifts represented the devotion of the heart. When David went to buy the ground on Mt. Zion which would become the location of the great Temple, the owner of that land, Araunah, offered to give David the land for free in honor of God. "The king replied to Araunah, 'No, I insist on paying you for it. I will not sacrifice to the LORD my God burnt offerings that cost me nothing.'" (2 Samuel 24:24) David insisted on paying 50 shekels of silver for that land, because if it didn't cost him something, he couldn't present it to God as an offering.

Of course, costliness is relative. A couple of turtle doves is as costly to a poor family as several bulls are to a rich one. God always accepted offerings on a sliding scale, recognizing the percentage of income they represented. That's why Jesus said that the poor widow who gave her eating money for the day had given more than all the others; she had given 100%. (cf. Luke 21:1-4)

Please do not suppose that religious offerings could somehow purchase God's favor; they could not. Our hearts are too impure for such offerings to ever be sufficient. Abel's offering was accepted only because he had faith in God's promise of salvation. That's why God later added other offerings to worship. The *sin offering* indicated that our sin must be covered by a substitutionary sacrifice. Old Testament sacrifices for sin pointed, of course, to Christ's work on our behalf. They declared that there is no salvation apart from His sacrifice. God also added *freewill offerings* that allowed His people to have holy and joyful parties, voluntarily celebrating their relationship with Him. These were feasts to which they invited the poor and destitute to rejoice with them in a God who never abandons us. But the central offering that defined worship was the *burnt offering*, the offering of one's substance to symbolize the intent of one's heart to manage everything exclusively for God's glory. The burnt offering was offered every day, morning and evening; it was the backbone of religious worship.

Tithing

Just how costly were those offerings supposed to be? What percentage of their income were God's people expected to devote to God? With Cain and Abel, we aren't told. With the patriarchs, there is no command. But something happened in the history of worship which did lead to a definite percentage. When God called Israel to be His nation, He developed a complete national religion. This included a Tabernacle designed to illustrate salvation by its very architecture, a priesthood to represent all His people living at His house, a host of sacrifices teaching the nature of redemption, and eventually a professional choir. Formal worship suddenly involved facilities, programs and staff. How was all this to be financed?

To provide financing for the religion God decreed, the Lord did something very gracious. He made a change in the way offerings to Him were handled. From that point on, only part of the offerings were to be burned, in many cases just a small part. God would take that small portion as representing the complete devotion of His people. He allowed the rest to finance the religion He had commanded. The bulk of the offerings would be used to build and maintain facilities, and support the Levites who worked there. The Levites had no inheritance of land in Israel; God was their inheritance, so the Lord deemed it appropriate to share His offerings with them.

Now that the offerings were expected to support the religion God designed, they had to be large enough to cover expenses. The Levites were an entire tribe, the Tabernacle or Temple needed maintenance, and some of the offerings still needed to be burned up completely…The net result: everyone's offering was to be ten percent of their income. Ten percent is called a *tithe*. Tithing was already an ancient voluntary custom, going back at least to Abraham. But at this point, it became the standard for everyone's worship because it made financial sense. From that point on in the Old Testament, a tithe was commanded of God's people as the minimum religious offering.

The tithe supported all the functions of expressing devotion, pointing to Christ, and celebrating Israel's salvation. Listen to one of the first descriptions of the tithe, "Eat…the tithe of your grain and new wine and oil…in the presence of the LORD your God at the place the LORD your God will choose—you, your sons and daughters, your menservants and maidservants, and the Levites from your towns—and you are to rejoice before the LORD your God in everything you put your hand to." (Deuteronomy 12:17-18) The tithe financed the joy of their religion, the joy of being called by God back into His family to worship Him with transformed lives.

The tithe was ten percent of their *gross* income. "A tithe of everything from the land, whether grain from the soil or fruit from the trees, belongs to the LORD; it is holy to the LORD." (Leviticus 27:30) The tithe came out of "the firstfruits of their grain, new wine, oil and honey and all that the fields produced...a tithe of everything." (2 Chronicles 31:5) *Firstfruits* implies that ten percent was taken "off the top." The tithe was separate from any charity a man gave to his neighbor. It was certainly distinct from any taxes levied by the king. One tenth of everything produced was holy to the Lord. How else could Israel finance their glorious religion and practice their stewardship of living all of life to the glory of God?

Before the cross, Jesus clearly supported the tithe. Like everything else, of course, He stressed that such outward behavior ought to flow out of inward faith. When he saw a Pharisee with a hardened heart tithing the herbs of his garden, He said, "Woe to you Pharisees, because you give God a tenth of your mint, rue and all other kinds of garden herbs, but you neglect justice and the love of God. You should have practiced the latter without leaving the former undone." (Luke 11:42) Give your heart to God first, and then the required religious tithe is acceptable.

Christian Offerings

After Jesus had fulfilled Old Testament symbolism through His cross and resurrection, the form of our religion changed. Since the purpose of the Temple was fulfilled, Christians abandoned the practice of burning up any portion of their offering to the Lord. In the early church, the focus was on using their gifts to support needy Christians. Of course, Christians also had to finance the expenses of their religion. But for many years they met in homes, so facility costs were down. They had to support their teachers, however. (1 Timothy 5:17-18) Most of all, they had a new mission: to reach the world with the gospel. That meant sending missionaries, and that would take as much money as they had vision to give.

Although generous giving is strongly taught (cf. 2 Corinthians 8-9), tithing is never mentioned. In the New Testament, religious offerings are more tied to need and to vision. Because of that, I believe it is inappropriate to say that the Bible requires Christians to tithe. The New Testament doesn't approach giving in terms of Israel's law. It assumes that Christians will voluntarily offer what is appropriate. Today, our offering demonstrates our passion for Christ and vision for ministry. Let each Christian give according to his or her own vision and passion. We do not teach that any particular percentage is required.

But I will say, as I have often said, that it is hard for me to understand how the vision and passion of any Christian could be less than that of anyone in the old covenant. For 2,000 years, the Lord did not think ten percent of our gross income too much to command. Could we seriously argue that our financial pressures are greater than those experienced by poor Israelite shepherds and farmers? How could the financing of our religion, including our houses of worship, ministry programs, pastoral and support staff, and *all* of missions call for less, now that Christ has come and opened the gospel to the whole world?

Christian, let's restore the offering as the central part of our formal, weekly worship. Let's practice our stewardship of all things by giving a portion of our income as an offering to God. Let's not think of it only as a collection to meet the church budget. God graciously allows us to use our gifts to Him for that purpose, but let's give our gifts as genuine religious offerings to express our stewardship of all things for His glory.

The question remains, however: How much should I give? I can't tell you that. I've told you how offerings developed in the Scriptures. I can't give you any laws about how much to give to the local church, and how much to other aspects or arms of the church.

I can say this, however: when it comes to our religion, you and I are responsible to give God our best. What is faith in God, if it does not give our best? In the Old Testament, God said, "'A son honors his father, and a servant his master. If I am a father, where is the honor due me? If I am a master, where is the respect due me?' says the LORD Almighty. 'When you bring blind animals for sacrifice, is that not wrong? When you sacrifice crippled or diseased animals, is that not wrong? Try offering them to your governor! Would he be pleased with you? Would he accept you?' says the LORD Almighty." (Malachi 1:6-8) Giving God leftovers when we worship Him is insulting. God responded to such an attitude, "'Oh, that one of you would shut the temple doors, so that you would not light useless fires on my altar! I am not pleased with you,' says the LORD Almighty, 'and I will accept no offering from your hands.'" (Malachi 1:10)

On the basis of that text, I would say that as a rule of thumb, our religious offering to God should be given *at least* the same attention that we give to our taxes. The point is not only one of obligation, but of simple respect and honor. I can't imagine any of us paying our taxes out of the loose change in our pockets, or with whatever we happen to find in our wallets. If you come to worship, and you approach the offering casually, with whatever is leftover and at hand, I urge you to please—for your own sake—stop right now. Stop giving altogether, stop insulting God, until you think things through. Be at least as respectful to God as you are to the IRS. At least budget your giving, and set your offering aside thoughtfully and purposefully. Let your financial offering be a genuine representation of your joy in knowing Christ.

Giving that Reflects our Faith

But what if I feel that I am not giving to the Lord an offering that matches my devotion and passion? I love Him more than my offering suggests. What can I do?

To begin with, please remember that God appreciates the *relative* cost of our offerings. Don't live in guilt because you cannot give as much as someone who is more wealthy. A given percentage of your income is less than that of richer folks, but it represents the same cost to God. A rich person must give a great deal to match the passion of the widow's two coins. God does not expect you to give what you do not have. When discussing giving, Paul advised us to give "according to [our] means. For if the willingness is there, the gift is acceptable according to what one has, not according to what he does not have." (2 Corinthians 8:11-12) Paul did not want people to give money to God one day, and then the next day be forced to borrow money from others to survive.

It would be superficial, however, to simply use our current lifestyle to determine the amount we can reasonably afford as an offering. Those who do not tithe probably cannot afford to do so, based on their current financial commitments. But, were taxes not factored into their budget, I'm sure they would not be able to "afford" them, either. We must adjust our lifestyle in order to honor our government and pay our taxes. We could certainly do the same to honor our Lord, if we understood our offering as worship, and not simply a collection.

If you want to increase your offering, you probably can. The first step is to learn to live by a budget, if you are not already. Budgeting brings discipline, understanding and satisfaction to our finances. One could argue that the ancient practice of tithing required God's people to learn to live life intentionally (on a budget). Budgeting is the easiest practical way to learn to make conscious priorities in life. If you need help, ask a friend or a church Deacon, or get a good Christian book on the subject.

Second, never believe you are too poor to increase your offering to God, if that is what you really want to do. You can always give a little bit more. If you want to give more, then set aside $10 more a month. If $10 is too much, then set aside $5. If $5 is too much, set aside $2. If it is your true desire to honor God by increasing your giving, then the discipline of actually laying aside an extra dollar or two will do more for your spirit than you can imagine. It will help you make your offering a priority, and when that happens, the amount will eventually sort itself out. Ask God for help in increasing your offering, and see what He does.

Consider giving in kind, with labor instead of money. Perhaps you can help take care of the church facility, or provide some service for a member of the church staff. Or perhaps you might set aside the money you would otherwise spend on a small luxury. Think what would it do for your sense of worship, if the money you gave was carefully planned and cultivated and put aside so you could devote it to Him!

What if my spouse and I can't agree on what to give as an offering? Pray and ask God for spiritual unity in your home—not about the offering, but first, about the faith that you share. Ask God for unity in worship and in the stewardship of your lives for Him, and once again, the amount you give will sort itself out. Don't argue about money at home. The only offering God accepts is one that is given joyfully, as an expression of devotion. (2 Corinthians 9:7) Focus on sharing the joy of your salvation, and let your offering rise to match your joy.

Worship Worth Passing On

Let me close with two things that really matter to me as a pastor. First, it is important to me that as believers, we learn to think of our offering as *worship*. I realize that the Lord would have us pay our church bills and meet our obligations, and I also realize that the days of the old altars are gone, so we can't really do what I am about to imagine. What I wish is that we could bring the offering plates to the front and set them on fire, consume every bill and melt down every coin, put a hole in the roof and let the smoke rise to God. We can't do that responsibly. But what we can do is rediscover how our offering dedicates our entire lives to Him. It can once again become a weekly testimony that I live, I exist, to manage all He gives me for His glory. As long as it's just a collection to pay the bills, we rob ourselves of what worship is supposed to be. Let's bring it forward as one of the high points in our worship.

Second, it is important to me that we teach our children how to worship. That means teaching them how to give offerings to the Lord. You don't think Cain and Abel thought up this on their own, do you? Their parents trained them. But recent polling shows that the proportion of younger adults who have never tithed and do not plan to, is growing. If young people are learning that it's OK to come before the Lord empty-handed, what kind of Lord are they learning about? And what kind of worship? Could our children even understand what David meant, when he said, "I will not give to the Lord my God offerings that cost me nothing"? David was a man after God's own heart; he *wanted* his worship to be costly. How are we going to leave behind a generation more spiritually passionate than ours, if we don't teach them how to give appropriate offerings to the Lord God?

Let's rediscover how our offerings form the very core of our formal worship. Our goal should not be to "meet our budget." Rather, may our budget have to increase in order to keep pace with our giving!

One day, we will stand before our Lord, saved entirely by grace, to receive assignments of responsibility for eternity. The Lord will remember our offerings, because they were gifts given to personally honor Him. To some of us, He will say, "Yes, I remember those gifts. They were like Abel's, so full of faith and devotion. I would like the whole earth to reflect that kind of devotion. Would you like to help lead that effort?...I thought you would!"

Prayer

Father, we have come a long way today, all the way from the first children of Adam and Eve, down to the present. It makes us wonder what worship will be like in paradise, in glory. Will we still come and offer you a portion of the fruit of our labor? Will we set it ablaze and watch it rise as a sweet aroma, or will we lay it at your feet? Or will the time for symbolism will be over, and our worship will truly consist of our work for you, day in and day out—all holy, all consecrated to your glory, just as it is.

We know we are not there yet. But we will not wait to taste paradise. We will taste it now, through the worship we offer when we gather together on the Sabbath. We will taste it through the offerings we dedicate to you together. What we offer, we offer in faith, through your Son, our Savior, who gave His body as a dying sacrifice on the cross, that we might offer ourselves as acceptable living sacrifices to you. Receive what we give, O Lord, for in Christ we give you our hearts. Amen.

Questions for Discussion

Genesis 4:3-7

Why do you think Abel and Cain offered some of the fruit of their labor to the Lord?

Why was Abel's offering accepted, and Cain's rejected?

What was the tithe?

Why do you think that amount was chosen by God?

How do you determine how much to give as a religious offering?

What do you teach your children about religious offerings?

What could you do—or what could your church do—to make the Sunday offering a more meaningful part of your worship?

The Faithful and Wise Manager

o o o o o o o o o o o o o o o o o o o o o o o o o o o o o o o o o o

"Be dressed ready for service and keep your lamps burning, like men waiting for their master to return from a wedding banquet, so that when he comes and knocks they can immediately open the door for him. It will be good for those servants whose master finds them watching when he comes. I tell you the truth, he will dress himself to serve, will have them recline at the table and will come and wait on them. It will be good for those servants whose master finds them ready, even if he comes in the second or third watch of the night. But understand this: If the owner of the house had known at what hour the thief was coming, he would not have let his house be broken into. You also must be ready, because the Son of Man will come at an hour when you do not expect him."

Peter asked, "Lord, are you telling this parable to us, or to everyone?"

The Lord answered, "Who then is the faithful and wise manager, whom the master puts in charge of his servants to give them their food allowance at the proper time? It will be good for that servant whom the master finds doing so when he returns. I tell you the truth, he will put him in charge of all his possessions. But suppose the servant says to himself, 'My master is taking a long time in coming,' and he then begins to beat the menservants and maidservants and to eat and drink and get drunk. The master of that servant will come on a day when he does not expect him and at an hour he is not aware of. He will cut him to pieces and assign him a place with the unbelievers."

—Luke 12:35-46

We began this study with one of Christ's parables teaching us that stewardship is finding joy in managing what God gives us for His glory. The study has focused on the things of eternal value that God has given us to manage: our bodies and minds, our children and neighbors, our planet and the church. It has also included the tools the Lord has given us to manage those things: our time, money and spiritual gifts. We gave the question of tithing special attention.

We end by going back to the beginning, or at least to another parable of Jesus that goes to the heart of stewardship. This one also stresses the motive behind living as stewards. What is it that makes stewardship work? What fuels it? We know that guilt is a poor motivator; it just doesn't work. Some would see self-control as the key to faithful management. But self-control needs a motive behind it, something that gives stewardship meaning and makes it worth the effort. The parable we studied at the beginning suggested that God is looking for servants who enjoy serving Him. We'll see that same theme echoed in this final study, as we examine the relational motives behind stewardship.

Word Pictures

Our text is not so much a single parable as it is a series of vignettes, word pictures strung together to develop an idea. First, Jesus paints the picture of a well-to-do home with a number of servants. The master is away for the evening at a wedding banquet. The way weddings worked in those days, after spending the day getting dressed and ready, the bride would be escorted by her attendants to the marriage supper. After she was settled, the bridegroom would be escorted to the feast by his friends, and the feast would begin. It could get quite late into the night—or the next morning—before the last guests left. In Jesus' little story, He mentions "the second or third watch of the night." In other words, the master could return home as early as 9 PM, or as late as 3 AM or later.

"Be dressed ready for service and keep your lamps burning, like men waiting for their master to return from a wedding banquet, so that when he comes and knocks they can immediately open the door for him." Lazy servants might very well go to sleep before the master returned. The oil lamps would go out, and the master would return to a dark, dismal home. He would have to knock loudly to wake up the servants, and they would keep him waiting at the door until they filled lamps with oil and got some light going. Then they would open the door bleary eyed, and the master would finally enter, having lost whatever joy he carried away from the banquet.

But good servants, who were delighted that their master was having a good time, would stay awake and keep lamps filled with oil. The master would come home to a cheerfully lit home and they would open up immediately. He would find his servants animated and interested to learn how things went. These servants love their master. They are his friends, as well as his servants. In fact, Jesus explicitly paints this friendship in vivid terms, "It will be good for those servants whose master finds them watching when he comes. I tell you the truth, he will dress himself to serve, will have them recline at the table and will come and wait on them."

Now, this sort of behavior is not very businesslike! Jesus describes here a very close household, indeed, one in which the master's joy spills over to everyone. In this scene, the master is still having such a good time that he doesn't want it to end. Instead of going to bed, he tells the servants to sit down and starts to serve them a late night snack. We can imagine the scene: with much laughter all around he continues the banquet. He describes the bride and groom, and goes over who was there, reviews the jokes and the sentiments shared. What a memorable evening. "It will be good for those servants whose master finds them watching when he comes." He is a master who likes being happy, and he likes to share his happiness with those around him. The servants who don't care about him, who sleep on the job or just go through the motions of service, will never know his happiness. They will never share it. In fact, it looks like they will be fired; the master has had enough of them. But how good it is for those servants who love their master so much that they gladly stay on the job as long as it takes, just to greet him when he comes home. They are in for a treat, because this is a master who enjoys sharing the happiness of his soul.

Is your Master a friend, whose service is a privilege? Or is He a bother, an interloper in his own house? Someone who gets in the way?

Jesus immediately paints another picture, also a nighttime scene, this time of a robber ready to pillage a home. Just like the returning master, the robber will arrive without warning, at any time. Those who are not prepared will find themselves destroyed, their wealth taken away and themselves, perhaps, killed.

Both parables deal with someone's unpredictable entrance upon the scene. That someone is Jesus, who is speaking here about His return. After His resurrection and ascension, Jesus will go away for a while. But He will come back, we don't know when. He is asking us, "Will you want to share my happiness when I come back? Or, will you greet me as a bother or as a thief, coming to assert my authority, or even steal, the life you feel belongs to you?"

When Jesus told these stories, Peter understood that Jesus was speaking to them, but he wondered whether Christ were speaking only to the Twelve? Peter asked, "Lord, are you telling this parable to us, or to everyone?" Jesus' answer is to paint some more pictures, indicating that these pictures are relevant for everyone, not just the apostles. They are questions He would ask of all who claim to follow Him. "Who then is the faithful and wise manager, whom the master puts in charge of his servants to give them their food allowance at the proper time? It will be good for that servant whom the master finds doing so when he returns. I tell you the truth, he will put him in charge of all his possessions. But suppose the servant says to himself, 'My master is taking a long time in coming,' and he then begins to beat the menservants and maidservants and to eat and drink and get drunk. The master of that servant will come on a day when he does not expect him and at an hour he is not aware of. He will cut him to pieces and assign him a place with the unbelievers."

This parable is very similar to the one with which we began our study. Here, the master is away, not for a night, but for many days or months. Once again, the issue is the attitude of the servants toward their master. Some treat him with no respect in his own home. They behave as if they own the house, and they own the other servants. You see this self-centeredness in the way they treat the property and the people; they act as if it all exists for them. Other servants realize that they are servants, and the master is…well…the *master*. They manage his property as he wishes. They enjoy the estate, but do so responsibly. They maintain the estate and treat other servants with the same respect and care as the master himself would.

Revealing the Heart

Jesus' point is that faithful stewardship while the master is away is a test that reveals what the servants really think of the master, and how they want the master to think of them. If you want to know what an employee thinks of you, see what he does and how he acts when you're away. If you want to know what a husband thinks of his wife, see what he does when he is on a business trip.

If you and I lived with Jesus, day in and day out, we would be on our very best behavior. But what about when Jesus is away? That's when the true nature of our faith in Him is revealed. Would we long for His return, living each day in faithful service, ready and hoping that we would hear Him knock at the door? Or would we want to take advantage of His absence by soaking up as much sin as we could before He returned like a thief to put an end to our fun?

We don't have to guess about our response; we demonstrate our response through our current stewardship of what He has entrusted to us. We are demonstrating it today, and every day. We either live as those for whom Christ is a bother, an intrusion in His own world, or we live hoping every day for His return so He can see our faithfulness in action. If the sky were to open in 90 seconds, good and faithful servants would not only be ready, they would be ecstatic. They wouldn't have to ask Him to wait a bit while they go and quickly take care of their responsibilities…quickly make out some checks to support things He wanted them to support, or quickly spend some more time with the kids before He evaluates their parenting, or quickly put their spiritual gifts to use. No, such servants wouldn't keep Him waiting a moment. They are "lights in the world" that have remained lit. They would want Him to find them just as they are, faithful in their stewardship.

Our stewardship in Jesus' absence is a test. It tests the quality of real faith, and exposes pretended faith. Many people are invited to serve in God's kingdom while it is being formed. As many as wish to, may come, whosoever will, may come, as many as confess the right words. Which of them really belongs in the kingdom when it is completed? Which of them really cares about God and His glory, and which of them really care most about themselves? Stewardship while the Master is away is a test. The results of this test are far-reaching. Servants who have no heart for their master are dismissed. They are punished to varying degrees for what they have stolen and for the way they have mistreated others, and they are cast out of the Master's house forever. Servants who delight in their service are given permanent positions in the master's house. Proportional to their delight, they are given positions of greater responsibility for eternal service. The good servant—the future steward—is motivated by love for the Master and hope in His return, when he will be found faithful.

When you understand that it is a test, then you can see that stewardship is not ultimately about the things we manage in this life at all. Ultimately, it's not about money or time or spiritual gifts. In the final analysis, it's not even about our care for the church, or the planet, or our neighbor, or our children, or even our minds and bodies. And it certainly isn't about rigorous tithing. *Stewardship is about what we really think of God, and how we long for Him to think of us.*

The natural human heart has been ruined by sin. It still works, it still thinks and feels and wills, but it has a ruined attitude toward God. The natural human heart does not trust the Living God who made us. It will only worship gods of our own making. It assumes the right to redefine god as it likes, so we remain in control of what we worship. We redefine God's laws according to what *we* believe will make us the most happy. "I know God doesn't mind me watching this trash because it helps me relax." "I'm sure God is OK with this purchase; I can always cut back on my offering." "I know God supports my decision to break up my children's home, because my wife doesn't make me happy anymore."

This idolatry is not evident in church services, where even those untouched by grace can still say the right words. It comes out in stewardship. Hearts untouched by grace demand ownership over all the stuff of life. Such household servants are out of place, treating the Lord as an intruder in His own house! He is not a master to wait up for, to greet with joy. He's a thief to fear, who might steal everything.

Good and faithful stewards have had a change of heart concerning God. They haven't only had a change of clothes, putting on the garb of a servant. They've had a change of heart, because through the Holy Spirit's grace they have discovered who God really is. For them, the cross is not just a password to get onto the payroll. It has convinced them that the Living God is worthy and wonderful.

The good and faithful steward has come to believe that there is no god better than the God of the Bible, the God revealed in Jesus Christ. We couldn't make up a better God. He is holy and righteous and altogether good. He is loving and kind and gracious beyond words. His laws may not be fun for hearts like ours that are still sick, in a world that is still sick, but we are convinced that His laws are best. We believe that He has our good at heart in all things. The good and faithful steward believes that the God we have discovered in Christ is worthy. He is worthy for everything to contribute to His glory—every cloud and mountain, every dollar bill, every second of time. The good and faithful steward is waiting expectantly for Christ's return. My life is His house. I want it lit up and ready for Him! I want Him glad to come home and find me here, waiting for Him with a big smile.

Stewardship not only has to do with what we think of God, but also how we long for God to think of us. The natural human heart is not only ruined, it is empty. There is a hole in it. That hole has to do with our meaning, our purpose, whether our life makes any positive difference in the scheme of things. We will use everything we've got to try and fill that hole before we die.

If your are like most people, and you want to find that hole in yourself quickly, all you have to do is think of your parents. Some few of us have had parents who were so nurturing and mature that they did a pretty good job filling that hole, but they are the rare exception. Most parents are just like us—immature, struggling so hard with their own issues that they don't have the wisdom or the energy to give their kids all they really need. They can give food and shelter and schooling, but children need so much more. Children need to know why they were born. They need help forming aspirations that are high and noble. They need even more help learning to live those aspirations. Children need so many things. But more than anything else, what children *long for* from parents is their honest, heartfelt approval. They need to know that their parents are glad they were born, and that they are proud of them.

God is our Father, so of course, the only thing that will ultimately fill the aching hole inside of each of us, is to hear our God say, "I'm proud of you." From God, "I'm proud of you" does not mean that sinners like us can earn His love. We cannot. What is means is that Jesus did His job well, and God the Father sees inside us a new, good heart recreated by His Holy Spirit—a heart that loves Him back. God can recognize when our faith is not a sham just to weasel into His house. He can see when it's real, when we trust Him, and know who He really is because we have recognized Him in His Son. It is a heart that beats for Him, that wants to be all He created us to be. When God sees His own face reflected off our heart, He is proud of it. He's so proud of what Jesus is making us to be. He's proud of us!

He Could Have Been Picturing You

Can you find yourself in this simple scene, as Jesus paints it with just a few words? Your master is away at the wedding banquet. He must be having a good time. It starts getting late, and some of the other servants begin getting edgy. They had some plans of their own for the evening that are being ruined—they have a life, too, you know. You just smile; you can wait up a little longer because you want to greet your master when he comes home.

It gets really late. Three of the other servants have gone to bed, and one is asleep in the kitchen. You take the lamps they were tending and fill them, too. You want the house lit up to welcome him home. You aren't just trying to get brownie points. This master took you in, and has been good to you. He's given you the run of his house and has entrusted to you the care of his family. It doesn't bother you to keep his things in good order. That's what you do, that's why you're here.

As you await his return, you ponder that he's the best person you've ever met. You've never considered service to him to be demeaning. In fact, since you live in his house, you live better than most who are on their own, and struggling to survive. You realize that the servant of a very important person is far more important than an unattached nobody. And it's not just that he is important; he is good. He is a good person. He's fair minded and wise. He treats everyone, including his servants, with respect, kindness and good humor. He is generous beyond all obligation. And he is willing to accept each servant as he or she is, not expecting more than they can give, and easily forgiving mistakes if the servant will honestly face them. As you sit there in the silence, you reflect that coming into his service, into his household, was the best thing that ever happened to you.

O, there he is, now, back from the wedding! You can hear him singing as he comes in the gate. You open the door for him. He greets you with a big grin and enters, dancing to music that still echoes in his soul. He starts bubbling over with news of the wedding, as you take his cloak and wash his feet. How beautiful the bride was, how happy the groom…the faces of both sets of parents…the pranks pulled by the younger siblings…who was there, and who wasn't…and the decorations…and all the food…He's far too excited and in too good a humor to go to bed. He asks you to fix up a little refreshment after his brisk walk.

While you get to work, he looks around and notices that you're the only one up. The servant who was sleeping in the kitchen awakens, runs his hand through his hair and offers to be of assistance. But the master says, "No, I think I have what I need. Go on to bed" and the man stumbles off.

You bring in some light refreshments, and as you set them down, you notice the master looking at you. Suddenly, with a grin, he tells you to sit down, and before you know what's happening, he swipes an apron off the wall and puts it on. Suddenly, your roles are reversed. You're sitting in the master's seat, a little embarrassed. But you can't help but laugh, because he's laughing. He has become your servant, pouring you a drink, slicing off some bread. He's having a grand time.

He sits down as the laughter subsides and you both eat a little, enjoying the quiet of those early morning hours. Finally, he says, "You know, I think I'm going to make a few changes around here."

"Oh?"

"Yeah, I've been watching what's been going on. I know how Rufus puts a little aside every time he pays the bills. And how Matilda puts a little away too…from the wine cellar. I'm aware of how Thaddeus throws his weight around with the rest of you, and finding Malcor asleep just now was no real surprise. They seem to feel like they own this place…but they don't. Tomorrow, they're going to be out on the street. I've had enough. In fact, I'm going to prosecute Rufus for theft."

The master goes on, "But my need for servants is only going to grow. My business is about to expand dramatically, you know. All my preparations are complete, and it's finally time to get started. I really need people I can depend on. I want a team with whom I can build something really great, a team to share it with." He pauses a second. "I'd like for you to head up that team, as my steward."

"Me?"

"Yes."

"Begging your pardon, sir, but we both know that Rufus is twice as good with numbers than I am, and Matilda is great with people. Thaddeus never gets tired and Malcor always has the right words…when he's awake." You smile.

"Yes, that's true." he says, also smiling, his eyes examining his plate, "But you see, you were the one who waited up for me tonight. You always wait up for me. You care about my house. You care about the people I love. You care about me. You don't embarrass my good name and you take care of things the way I want. You're the kind of servant I'm looking for in a steward."

"The fact is," he continues, "the others treat me like a stranger in my own home. But you, you're more than just a servant." Now he's looking right at you. "You're my friend. You treat me with the respect and love due a father. And I think you know I feel that same way toward you, like you were my child. I'm proud of you."

After a long moment, he says, "Look, when the others leave tomorrow, let's spend the day talking about our future."

Christian, that's the conversation I want to have at Christ's return. It motivates my life in a way that guilt or naked self-discipline never could. It makes me wait for Him, hoping each day that He will return to find me faithful.

Stewardship is finding joy in managing all God gives us for His glory. Salvation is a gift, pure and simple. But stewardship is a test. It is motivated by how we think of God, and how we want Him to think of us. It is sustained by the hope that one day our service will be evaluated and found faithful, leading to the words every Christian wants to hear, "Well done, good and faithful servant. You have been faithful with a few things; I will put you in charge of many things. Come and share your master's happiness!"

Prayer

Father, Jesus' pictures are so rich and wonderful, they are hard to believe. That we would be proud of you makes sense. You deserve our pride. Being proud of you feels right. But for you to be proud of us? We, whose sin is worthy of your condemnation? We, whose best efforts of service and worship are impure?

The thought of you being pleased with us sends a chill up our back. It is what we long for, down deep. We thought that our sin had made such fatherly pride impossible, that all we could ever hope for from you would be a disappointed grace, as Jesus makes up for all our failings.

We forget about the new heart your Holy Spirit crafts inside of those who know your Son. We forget that our new heart is His craftsmanship that prepares us to do good things that please you.

So, Father, we will focus today on what you have entrusted to us to manage for you: our bodies and minds, our children and our neighbor, our planet and your church. And we will concentrate on using our time and money and spiritual gifts to manage those things well. Out of gratitude for your unmerited grace, we will work hard, looking forward to the day when we can lay the results before you, see your satisfaction and receive our assignments for eternity. And we will do it in Jesus' name. Amen.

Questions for Discussion

Luke 12:35-46

Contrast the attitudes and expectations of the various servants waiting for the master to return from the wedding banquet.

Why will Jesus' return be positive for some, but negative for others?

In the ancient world, masters never waited upon servants. What do you think Jesus is trying to tell us, through this surprising promise?

How is the image of being surprised by a thief relevant?

Jesus makes a second contrast concerning those who are supposed to be serving Him.

Contrast the servants described in response to Peter's question.

What do their respective fates say about how Jesus will respond when He returns?

What do you think it means, that God will put trusted servants in charge of all His possessions?

What is God looking for in a future steward of His kingdom?

978-0-595-35492-4
0-595-35492-0

Printed in the United States
30113LVS00002B/59

9 780595 354924